UNFU*K
YOUR LIFE

Achieve Success and Peace
in 30 Days on Your Own

ASLAN MIRKALAMI

10-10-10
Publishing

Unfu*k Your Life: Achieve Success and Peace in 30 Days on Your Own

Copyright © 2019 Aslan Mirkalami

ISBN: 978-1-77277-306-4

Limits of Liability and Disclaimer of Warranty

The author and publisher shall not be liable for your misuse of the enclosed material. This book is strictly for informational and educational purposes only.

Warning – Disclaimer

The purpose of this book is to educate and entertain. The author and/ or publisher do not guarantee that anyone following these techniques, suggestions, tips, ideas, or strategies will become successful. The author and/or publisher shall have neither liability nor responsibility to anyone with respect to any loss or damage caused, or alleged to be caused, directly or indirectly by the information contained in this book.

Medical Disclaimer

The medical or health information in this book is provided as an information resource only, and is not to be used or relied on for any diagnostic or treatment purposes. This information is not intended to be patient education, does not create any patient-physician relationship, and should not be used as a substitute for professional diagnosis and treatment.

Publisher
10-10-10 Publishing
Markham, ON
Canada

Printed in Canada and the United States of America

DEDICATION

I dedicate this book to my magnificent granddaughter, Siana Mirkalami, for her incredible strength and willingness to not give up in the face of adversity. May her life be full of beautiful experiences, excitement, and happiness.

TABLE OF CONTENTS

FOREWORD

As public speakers, teachers, coaches, and in some case healers, we all bring a unique expertise and set of tools within our tool kits that we share with people around the word, so that we may help them to make positive changes in their lives.

However, what differentiates Aslan's book from many others in the self-help market is that he teaches you to engage with your unconscious mind, facilitating changes to actualize at the unconscious level. As our unconscious mind is the most powerful force to get in the way of your goal achievement, it is also the most important tool to engage with, as it allows you to make crucial changes at the source level.

This powerful work will help you to repair wounds around your past decisions, disappointments, hurts, and traumas so that you do not continue to carry the shame, blame, guilt, or pain from events and relationships that have transpired throughout your life. As a result, this pivotal work is freeing, as the practical skills that Aslan teaches, will empower you to finally move forward with a new, unencumbered, lease on life.

Aslan shares his unique set of talents and systems that he has honed over his 12-year coaching career. Although the practices are somewhat advanced, Aslan writes in an impactful, straightforward, and simple language so that anyone can understand what he is teaching.

In fact, this is one of the most effective self-help books you will ever read, because Aslan teaches you to not only engage with your unconscious mind, but also to partner with it to make changes that you want to manifest in your life. By following the steps laid out in the book, you will be able to achieve the results that you are looking for.

Often referred to by his clients as "the Results Doctor," Aslan shares his coaching expertise so that you can use the techniques on your own, saving you thousands and thousands of dollars in coaching costs. Aslan sees himself as a master change agent, as in a very short period of time, he is able to help his clients reach substantial goals, setting them on the path to reach their full potential.

Dedicated to helping his clients achieve their best lives, Aslan wrote this book as a gift to his children, to ensure that they are able to achieve the results in their lives that he has.

Aslan Mirkalami's *Unfu*k Your Life: Achieve Success and Inner Peach in 30 Days on your Own*, will provide you with invaluable tools, techniques, and tactics to use throughout your life so that you can achieve anything your heart and mind desire!

Raymond Aaron
New York Times Bestselling Author

ACKNOWLEDGEMENTS

My mom, (Fatemeh), for loving me and instilling in me a strength of character. You were my rock.

To my son, (Alexander), and daughter, (Joyse), who have brought joy to my life that I did not know was possible. It's been amazing to watch you grow up into loving, generous, and kind people. I am, and will remain, forever proud of who you are in this world.

Bob Proctor, a mentor of mine, for inspiring me to not limit myself in life, with his *You Were Born Rich* program.

Mr. Kabock was the first person to turn me on to a life of personal development and achievement.

Vern Woolf was a mentor, confidant, and a wizard. Thank you for creating a safe space for me to unwind, and for inspiring me to live to my fullest potential.

John Grinder, for being a mentor, confidant, wizard, and friend. Thank you for honest straightforward communication. But more importantly, thank you for sharing your genius with the world, and for allowing me to be witness to your genius.

Richard Bandler, for being a mentor, teacher, wizard, and friend.

Tony Robbins, for being an instrument of personal change in my life.

Stephen Gilligan, thank you for being such a compassionate, loving friend, and for showing me how to heal parts of myself that would have likely remained unhealed.

Oprah Winfrey, thank you for being an incredible inspiration and a demonstration of how we can come from nothing and make something great in our lives. From you, I have learned how to manifest my dreams.

Dr. Mehmet Oz, thank you for being a source of inspiration for me. You taught me that it doesn't matter where you come from. You can always be great in America.

INTRODUCTION

I wrote this book as a gift to my children, as I wanted them to have tools to create a life that is limitless. I wanted them to be able to repair any wounds or conflicts, and eradicate negative self-beliefs that could hold them back in life. Further, I wanted them to feel a sense of freedom, have control over their choices, and create successful lives that they are proud of.

I also wrote this book because of the hundreds of clients that I have helped through my coaching business over the past 12 years. Being witness to their incredible transformations has inspired me to help more people on a larger scale.

I am excited to share a system with you, which teaches you to engage and partner with an incredibly powerful force, the unconscious mind, to make substantial changes in your life. The best part about it—it is FREE! And you can utilize the tools and techniques at any time or place. There are no limits. Can you imagine?

Why communicate and partner with the unconscious mind? Simply because the unconscious mind is an expert saboteur, wreaking havoc in all areas of your life, without your knowledge. However, after reading this book, and following the exercises, you will know how to work in harmony with this tremendous resource.

The exercises will help you to make pivotal decisions in your life, in regard to your relationships, career, and finances. Moreover, you will be able to detect the conflicts in your body, and use the unconscious mind to help you to create a harmonious environment, free from illness and disease. So, whether it's getting over past hurt, disappointment, or trauma, or overcoming financial problems, or whether you are suffering with medical issues, this book will provide you with the tools and techniques to help you create a life you love!

The definition of insanity is doing the same thing over and over again, and expecting a different result. Well, I'm here to offer you a NEW way of doing things, so that you can achieve NEW, mind-blowing results.

If you are ready to create meaningful and lasting changes in your life, I implore you to keep reading. But first, close your eyes and dream of the possibilities....

What do you want your life to look like? Visualize your future, with details that you can almost taste, feel, hear, see, and smell.

Now you are ready to begin your wondrous transformational journey.

1

Are You Really Fu*ked?

"*I* am not what
happened to me;
I am what I choose
to become."

– Carl Jung

I realize that the title of this book, *Unfu*k Your Life: Achieve Success and Inner Peace in 30 Days on Your Own,* is quite provocative. I am aware that the language may even turn you off. That's okay, because I am here to WAKE YOU UP! After all, there is a reason you picked up this book and chose to read it. You are looking for a much-needed change in your life, and you are hoping that the words on the following pages will inspire you.

However, the pages in this book will not inspire you to jump up and declare a new path in life, as I am not here to motivate you. Nor will I shame you into making new to-do lists or plans. Instead, throughout this book, I am going to share information with you that may be shocking or difficult to comprehend, and at times painful to admit about yourself.

I ask that you stick with me, because if you do, you will be able to create a powerful transformation in your life—one that you could not believe was possible. You will learn to work in harmony with the powerful forces that, until now, have led you down the wrong path.

Why do I want to help you? Because it is my greatest joy in life to help people become who they are supposed to be. To witness a change in their lives that empowers them to a new level of being and consciousness, and to observe them evolve into powerful forces in their own lives—well, there is no greater joy. And I want that for you. Truly.

Through my transformative coaching practice, I have helped dozens of people make real change. And I believe, with every core of my being, that I can do the same for you, which brings me to an important question that I want you to consider.

I want you to get prepared to experience a moment of truth. Some may call it a *come to Jesus* moment that may leave you feeling horrible about yourself. But before you ask yourself this critical question, be prepared for what you discover, as the path to enlightenment is through the truth.

What is so fu*ked about your life?

If, after asking yourself this honest question about the current state of your life, you find yourself experiencing strange or painful sensations in your body as you acknowledge your truth, I ask you to be honest, and name it. It is not the time for denial—that is another book! Write down your thoughts. Journal. Emote. Express. And feel.

If you are unsure about the path that has led you to me, be assured that I will share examples of everyday people who were once unhappy, broke, and sick, to name a few, which may sound familiar to you. After all, why are you reading a book entitled *Unfu*k Your Life*?

But first I will present you with some troubling data that represents the current state of our society. It's alarming, so if you are aware that you need to make serious changes in your life, and you do not need convincing, you can go straight to the section in this chapter, entitled "What Is Your Happiness Factor?"

IS YOUR RELATIONSHIP IN TROUBLE?

Perhaps you are unhappy in your relationship or marriage. That's not a surprise, as according to the National Center for Health Statistics and U.S. Census Bureau, in the past 25 years, leading up to 2015, the divorce rate had almost doubled for those aged 50 and older. And for those younger than age 50, the divorce rate is near twice the rate of their older counterparts.[1]

Did you know that if you have a close friend or relative who is divorced, then your chances of also getting divorced increases? Crazy as it sounds, according to a recent study, divorce is contagious. According to Pew Research, after analyzing three decades of Massachusetts data on marriage, divorce, and remarriage, Brown University researchers found that "study participants were 75% more likely to become divorced if a friend is divorced, and 33% more likely to end their marriage if a friend of a friend is divorced." Veritably, it can affect friends up to two degrees of separation. This *social contagion* is spread through information, attitudes, and behaviors that are shared among people in one's personal and social networks. [2]

Divorce is contagious! Who knew?

---

1   https://www.pewresearch.org/fact-tank/2017/03/09/led-by-baby-boomers-divorce-rates-climb-for-americas-50-population/

2   https://www.pewresearch.org/fact-tank/2013/10/21/is-divorce-contagious/

ARE YOU PART OF THE SOUL-CRUSHING RAT RACE?

If you are feeling pretty confident about your romantic relationship, then perhaps you are unhappy in a job that does not fulfill you. Steve Jobs says, *"The only way to do great work is to love what you do. If you haven't found it yet, keep looking. Don't settle."*

If you are one of those unfortunate people who hate their job, then you are carrying toxic energy in your body, and internalizing it into your cells. According to *Psychology Today*, "the mind-body connection between stress and our physical health is clear: Stress on the inside causes stress to manifest on the outside." The article goes on to say that to cope with the stress, people self-medicate "with food, alcohol, nicotine, caffeine, or prescription or illegal drugs."[3] Later in the book, I will discuss how carrying this negative energy in your body wreaks havoc on your nervous system.

Stanford Graduate School of Business Professor, Jeffrey Pfeffer, wrote in his 2018 book, *Dying for a Paycheck: How Modern Management Harms Employee Health and Company Performance—and What We Can Do About It*, that "in one survey, 61 percent of employees said that workplace stress had made them sick, and 7 percent said that they had actually been hospitalized." He goes on to write that "job stress

---

3   https://www.psychologytoday.com/us/blog/the-act-violence/201409/why-toxic-people-drive-you-mad

costs US employers more than $300 billion **annually,** and may cause 120,000 excess deaths each year. In China, 1 million people a year may be dying from overwork. People are dying for a paycheck. And it needs to stop."[4]

If you don't think your job is killing you, then that is excellent news! However, if your current job does not light you up in the morning, or get you jumping out of bed, perhaps you are like millions of other people who daydream of making a bold career change. These feelings are not surprising, as it is becoming all too commonplace. So, whether it's early retirement packages that have allowed people to re-think how they want to spend their 7+hours each day, or the millions of people who have fallen into their current career, change is the new normal.

And although career changes seem popular among millennials to baby boomers, the United States Bureau of Labor Statistics does not have any reliable data on the number of career changes over one's lifetime, as they are unable to define what career change is.[5] What did we learn? Jobs can create stress in our bodies, which can make us sick. Therefore, it is essential to live by these famous words (often wrongly

---

4   https://www.amazon.com/Dying-Paycheck-Management-Employee-Performance/dp/0062800922

5   https://www.bls.gov/nls/nlsfaqs.htm#anch43

attributed to Confucius): **"Find something you love to do, and you'll never have to work a day in your life."** [6]

ARE YOUR FINANCES A MESS?

Maybe you are happy with the line of work that you are in, but you are sick and tired of living paycheck to paycheck. Who isn't?

Since Bernie Sanders, 2016 presidential candidate, talked about the 1% and the wealth disparity that we live with, it has been all over the media.

What is wealth disparity? In the United States, capitalism is alive and well, as they produce more global millionaires than any other country. The top 1 percent of wealthy Americans hold almost 43% of the national wealth, which far exceeds other OECD countries. Moreover, according to Inequality.org, the "world's richest 1 percent, those with more than $1 million, own 45 percent of the world's wealth. Adults with less than $10,000 in wealth make up 64 percent of the world's population but hold less than 2 percent of global wealth." [7]

People are angry and fed-up, as they often feel like they have no way to overcome the overwhelming odds against them. The truth is,

---

6   https://quoteinvestigator.com/2014/09/02/job-love/

7   https://inequality.org/facts/global-inequality/

with a global problem as severe and complex as wealth disparity, there seems to be no quick fix.

IS YOUR HEALTH IN PERIL?

If you consider yourself lucky for being successful in many areas of your life, such as career and relationships, then I am happy for you. However, if you are like millions of others, who are plagued with chronic illness, or worse, a serious disease, then I'm here to tell you that there may be hope in changing your outcomes.

Most people are out of shape or overweight. They don't take care of themselves. According to *Fortune Magazine*, "More than 70% of Americans are now either obese or overweight by this measure. However, the statistics are particularly worrying. Almost 40% of adults are obese. The childhood obesity rate, for ages 6–19, has increased to 20%."[8] (Oct. 13, 2017)

The sheer number of people worldwide that are overweight or obese is an epidemic. The Worldwide Health Organization claims that obesity has nearly tripled since 1975, with over 1.9 billion adults (18 years and older) being overweight, and over 650 million of them

---

8   http://fortune.com/2017/10/13/obesity-in-america/

being obese.[9] Given the significant risk factors for chronic diseases, such as diabetes, cardiovascular diseases, and cancer, this is a huge issue that needs to be addressed, from a systemic level to a personal one (through lifestyle changes).

HOW IS YOUR MENTAL HEALTH?

If physical health, or the lack thereof, is not enough to have us shaking in our boots, the U.S. Department of Health and Human Services, National Institute of Mental Health, states that major depression is one of the most common mental disorders in the United States. Major depressive disorder can be debilitating, causing a person to experience symptoms such as a loss of interest or pleasure in daily activities, and problems with sleeping, eating, energy level, focus, concentration, or sense of self-worth. In 2017, an estimated 17.3 million adults over age 18, living in the USA, were diagnosed with at least one major depressive episode. An estimated 65% of these adults were treated with a combination of counseling and medication.[10]

Like millions of other people across the USA, do you rely on antidepressants and stimulants such as caffeine to get you through

9   https://www.who.int/news-room/fact-sheets/detail/obesity-and-overweight

10 https://www.nimh.nih.gov/health/statistics/major-depression.shtml

the day? If so, you are NOT alone. The fact is that most people are unhappy with themselves or their position in life.

Harvard Health Publishing reported on statistics from the National Center for Health Statistics (NCHS), which are quite alarming. Antidepressant usage amount teens and adults "increased by almost 400% between 1988–1994, and 2005–2008." Furthermore, American health statisticians estimate that one in every ten Americans take antidepressants. One in ten! No wonder it is a billion-dollar industry![11]

In 2017, *TIME Magazine* reported that clinical depression affects about 16 million people in the United States. Additionally, depression is responsible for an estimated $210 billion a year in lost productivity, and health care needs.[12]

As a result, antidepressants are projected to grow globally to nearly $17 billion by 2020—the pharmaceutical industry is mammoth. Therefore, it's no wonder that big-pharma rakes in billions of dollars by keeping us sick—or by having us believe that we are sick. More

---

11 https://www.prnewswire.com/news-releases/antidepressant-drugs-market-to-reach-15-98-bn-by-2023-globally-at-2-1-cagr-says-allied-market-research-873540700.html

12 http://time.com/4900248/antidepressants-depression-more-common/

about the impact of mental illness, and what we can do about it, will be covered in later chapters.[13]

Bob Green, the acclaimed author, and Oprah Winfrey's go-to trainer, says that *"the body achieves what the mind believes."* If our bodies and minds are plagued with illness, it is only natural to doubt if we can be healed. But I am here to tell you, "YES!"

WHAT IS YOUR HAPPINESS FACTOR?

The fact is that people are unhappy. According to Shawn Achor, who studied happiness for over ten years at Harvard University, *"ninety percent of our happiness is not based on the external world but the lens through which you view it."* Achor teaches that you create happiness merely by changing the lens.[14] I will show you how to *change the lens*, or to change your paradigm.

Sadly, most people feel like they are failing. Or worse, they feel like complete failures. There is a distinction, however. The former is how people currently feel. There is some hope in that they believe if they change their actions or behaviors, then they will feel happy. However, the latter is an overall feeling of failure. Everything they do or say, or

---

13 https://www.health.harvard.edu/blog/astounding-increase-in-antidepressant-use-by-americans-201110203624

14 https://www.texasmonthly.com/articles/shawn-achor/

have done or said, for the most part, is a failure—what a horrible way to go through life.

It's the difference between parents calling out a child's *behavior* as bad, versus calling the *child* bad. Both feel horrible for the child. But being called *bad,* by their mom or dad, scars that child for life. Do you see the difference? One is internalized more than the other, and is consequently carried with us throughout our lives.

At one of my workshops, I asked a group of 500 people to raise their hand if they felt they were living the life they always wanted. Sadly, not one person raised their hand—not one.

"One of the most powerful forces in human nature is our belief that change is possible."

– Shawn Achor

WHO IS IN CHARGE?

Who are you? What role do you actively play in your success and failure? How often are you conscious?

Scientists are now telling us that although our eyes may be open, and *the lights are on*, people are not conscious. We are either daydreaming or planning something to happen in the future; or we are conditioned to do things out of habit, automatically.

We are creatures of habit. Think about it. Do you need to remind yourself what hand to use when you brush your teeth? No, this is an example of an unconscious habit at work, which is okay. After all, if the unconscious mind wants to help us perform regular activities that we don't want to exert brain power over, such as brushing our teeth, what is the harm? Well, the harm could be the fundamental fact that the unconscious mind has its own agenda. Think about it. Who, or what, is controlling our actions?

Digest that concept for a moment, as it is vital for your ability to transform your life. The unconscious mind has an agenda. Most of the time, you are not in control of it. What does that mean? Should you be scared? No, **but if you want to make momentous changes in your life, which I know you are capable of, I want you to admit that until you become enlightened, your life is fu*ked.**

How do you become enlightened? How do you connect with your unconscious mind? You will learn the answers to these questions as we progress through the book.

Who, or what, is in charge? Is it your conscious self or your unconscious self? Most people are unaware. They are not paying attention to who is in control, and end up one day feeling like their life is a mess. Does this sound like you? Are your relationships in turmoil, your finances in crises, or is your health failing you? It's no wonder!

Many successful people have categorized their goals and laid out specific action items and targets to meet along the way. They have well-thought-out plans, particular deliverables, and daily reminders, and they visualize what they want to achieve. They have systems in place to hold themselves accountable, and appear to be making all of the right moves. One would think that this *successful person* has it all. They are, after all, *living the dream*. But—and I am sorry to burst your celestial bubble—our unconscious mind is playing a puppet show for us, entertaining us, and tricking us into believing that we are making these decisions.

This puppet show is so convincing that we look at *models of perfection*—such wealthy, beautiful, and famous role models—that we wish to emulate. We inevitably believe that their success was a result of their choices and actions.

However, we are NOT the master of our universe. Instead, we are entangled in our paradigm, which moves us without us knowing, and without us paying attention. We become entangled emotionally, and spiritually, and we believe in things that are not real. This belief often leads us to ask if we have free will.

Scientists and everyday people think that we do not have free will. Beliefs such as this make sense, since people often do not continue to do what is needed to attain it. However, I believe that like the successful one percent of the population, we can acquire free will. There is a way to become in charge of your life experiences and, ultimately, your destiny.

You, too, can shift your paradigm if you are open to the idea, and willing to do the work.

DO YOU GIVE IN AND PLAY A VICTIM?

What role do you play in life? How about the people with whom you surround yourself?

Author and behavioral scientist, Steve Maraboli, says, *"The victim mindset produces a delusion of fault and blame that blames you from the simple truth of cause and effect."*

Do you know someone who often plays the victim? Regardless of the circumstances, the problem is always someone else's fault. Perhaps you play the victim card to excuse the sorry state of your life. This type of victim attitude is a result of thinking that external events are responsible for the unfortunate things happening in your life. What do I mean by this? One example of this is impoverished people blaming rich people for their financial woes.

Rich people, otherwise known as the 1%, become financially successful regardless of your financial situation. Believe it or not, there is no real correlation between your poverty and Jeff Bezos' (owner of Amazon) wealth. So, while your mild obsession with buying things on Amazon is getting in the way of your goal to save money, Mr. Bezos is not responsible for your dismal bank balance. Likewise, rich people are not responsible for your financial choices, spending habits, or low income that you make at your lousy job.

Sorry for the tough love here, but coddling you is not going to help you transform your life—nor is complaining about the rich. While I agree that the wealth disparity that exists in the United States, and around the world, is not fair, it is what it is.

According to Greg Satal, of *Harvard Business Review*, *"on September 17, 2011, Occupy Wall Street took over Zuccotti Park, in the heart of the financial district in Lower Manhattan."* The protesters' goal was to vilify corporate leaders and bring awareness to the wealth disparity among the rich (the 1%) and the poor (the 99%). While their protest captured the attention of the nation, and inspired others around the world to organize their demonstrations on a global day of protest, the poor remain poor, and the wealthy stay rich.[15]

Again, it is not the wealthy 1% who are responsible for your financial failures. Still not convinced? Let's transition this to something more relatable, such as love and relationships, and if you were utterly envious of a couple that was sick in love with each other. Their love and affection, evident to the world, would have them die for each other. Let's pretend for a moment that they both died. Would their tragic death make your relationship better? Of course not—because what happens in the relationships of others does not have an impact

---

15 https://web.archive.org/web/20140331062327/http://newsfeed. time.com/2011/10/17/solidarity-saturday-occupy-wall-street-goes-global/

on our relationships. Likewise, rich people's wealth does not affect your finances.

Knowing this, we need to accept that only we are responsible for the success in our lives. Blaming something, or someone, is blaming external forces. But what if you changed the paradigm and looked inward instead? Would this shift put you in control of the situation? Whether it's wealth, health, or love, only YOU can drive forward significant changes and transformation in your life. To live as a victim is to give in.

DO YOU FIGHT?

How do you define yourself? Are you a fighter? A survivor? A winner?

The other way to live your life is to push back. However, fighting can be exhausting and not net you the results you seek. For example, if you tried to fight an elephant, you would use all of your muscles and might, but to no avail, and you would lose. The elephant would drag you and likely crush you to death. Your fight would be for naught.

Society often views fighters and survivors as winners, which is understandable—especially if someone has overcome horrible circumstances, or worse, horrific tragedy. But again, fighting exerts a tremendous amount of energy, and wreaks havoc on your nervous system.

Perhaps fighting an elephant is a glaring example of knowing that you are doomed to fail. After all, how powerful are you? The real question is how powerful your unconscious mind is. The unconscious mind is, of course, less intelligent, but it is way more powerful.

According to a former professor of medicine at Stanford University, Dr. Bruce Lipton, the unconscious mind is in control, compelling us to operate in automatic mode, a whopping 95% of the time! Lipton's study teaches us that the unconscious mind is one million times more powerful than the conscious mind. Moreover, it's running on autopilot, 95–99% of the time.[16]

Take poverty, for example. Because you cannot fight against your unconscious mind, it becomes convinced that you need to be poor. Your unconscious mind says that you do not deserve wealth because you are not worthy (These internalized and unconscious beliefs likely stem from your childhood.). Your unconscious mind will not allow you to succeed, and therefore, it robs you of opportunities to achieve success. It makes you look bad to others, feel like you are a failure, and think that you were in control of the adverse decisions that put you into this financial state. However, you were not in control of those choices.

---

16 http://www.lifetrainings.com/Your-unconscious-mind-is-running-you-life.html

The truth is, when you remain unaware of your unconscious mind at work, you allow it to become an expert saboteur in your life! Who needs enemies when you have a naughty unconscious mind at work!

Wow! It is no wonder that positive thinking, affirmations, and sheer will alone do not fix what's broken in our lives! No worries, though, as I have helped dozens of clients to get their lives back on track. This book is about gaining wisdom and becoming enlightened. I have taught my clients to take control of their nervous systems and, ultimately, gain control over their lives. Within a short period, they come to understand that they are entirely in charge. They become the center of their universe.

> *"Once we trace the conflicts, and turn them into harmony, all your resources will be available to your body, and your body will know what to do."*
>
> **– Aslan Mirkalami**

One of my one-to-one clients, a 40-year-old woman named Sara, came to me with severe scoliosis, a curvature of the spine, often caused by the *nervous system (*the *brain,* spine, and nerves). Her goal was to have a baby. However, with a 70-degree curvature, Sara's doctors recommended surgery to fix her back so that she could carry a baby to term. I worked with her, using the methods and concepts outlined in the book, and a year later, her curvature improved enough for her to get pregnant. I share this success story with you, not to say that I am a miracle worker or a doctor—because I am not—but to show you that what I taught Sara was to heal herself using her unconscious mind.

Another example is one of my elite one-to-one clients, Joshua, who came to see me for help to heal his arm. He lost an inch of his forearm's main bone due to a shooting that occurred when he lived in Ecuador. The surgeons worked to repair Joshua's arm, but he, unfortunately, contracted a bacterial infection in his bone marrow. His doctors wanted to amputate his arm, as the infection was quite severe and could spread to the rest of his body. Joshua was taking an enormous amount of antibiotics to prevent the infection from spreading. However, we did intense work together, and after a week, Joshua's redness and inflammation in his arm went away. Later, his doctor did a scan to confirm that all of the infection had cleared, and it had!

Now, to be clear, I am not claiming to be a doctor or a healer extraordinaire. However, through my work, I have helped my clients to achieve remarkable results such as Sara's and Joshua's. Some may call it miracles. However, I claim to teach you how to manifest the healing, versus manifesting the disease. All I can say is that once we trace the conflicts, and turn them into harmony, all your resources will be available to your body, and your body will know what to do. So, your body becomes the miracle—not me.

YOUR IDENTITY – DO YOU CREATE A NECESSITY TO FIT IN?

We often become different versions of ourselves, depending on who we are with. Which version of you is real? Which version is authentic?

People create an identity out of the necessity to fit in. We form our identity for others because we want to fit into society. We want to ensure that our behavior is consistent so that people know where we stand, what we have to offer, and where we fit in. People like to put others into neat little boxes or buckets, to distinguish themselves from others, and to identify with others. This necessity to fit in begins from our family of origin.

When we are first born, we are made of 100% pure love. Our very being is the product of love. No matter what we do as infants, such as poop or pee on ourselves (or our parents), we are praised by how amazing and precious we are. Still, somewhere around the tender age of two or three, our parents begin to tame us. They tame us through punishment and withdrawing love—or we are called bad or wrong. You see, these adults want us to behave like them. They want us to fit into the existing family structure, and to join their harmonious relationship.

But what once was unconditional love turns into conditional love. We grow up believing that our parents will love us if we are like them, and if we do what they say. It becomes the basis of our life, which messes us up because we learn that to be loved, we need to be what someone else wants us to be.

It's the foundation of us feeling like we are not loved, or that we are wrong. Most people feel unloved, unworthy, and undeserving. Consciously though, they would say that they don't think that way about themselves. However, once they go deep into our work, and they start focusing on some parts of their childhood, their language changes. They start telling me negative things that their conscious selves would never share with me. When we are working together, I often hear them say horrible things, such as calling themselves *pathetic*, or worse.

To fit in, it comes down to identity. If we lived alone in the world, we would have no identity, because there would be no one else to define us and to put us into a box that makes them comfortable.

DO YOU PARTNER?

Oprah Winfrey says that *"When you undervalue what you do, the world will undervalue who you are."*[17]

Society, the media, and the people in our lives are continually telling us that we are not good enough. Is that why we were so desperate to believe Mark Darcy when he proclaimed to Bridgette, in the

---

17 http://www.thinking-minds.net/10-success-tips-oprah-winfrey/

blockbuster movie, *Bridget Jones' Diary,* "*I like you very much, just as you are?*" That is wishful thinking.

From a young age, we are conditioned to look and act a certain way. Parents, older siblings, teachers, community leaders, and peers tell us that we are not good enough. We are not smart enough, or attractive enough, or tall enough, or kind enough. Everywhere we look, others are judging us—so much so, that as we age, we begin to internalize all of the negative messages that we heard growing up.

So, while you may *present* to the world that you have it together, on the inside, you feel like a mess. You question your choices, your relationships, your goals, and your accomplishments. Your homes are not beautiful enough; your car is not fancy enough; your kids are not well-behaved enough.

All of these messages reinforce your belief that you are not enough. It's like the cake was baked when we were children—when our parents were trying to mold us into replicas of themselves, or better versions of themselves. Then, as we went through life, others around us made us feel even worse about who we are.

Does it ever stop? If we didn't allow ourselves to become tortured by all of the negative *stuff* coming at us, it would be bearable. But the truth is, we believe the crap. We believe that we are unworthy, unlovable, or unkind—the *un's* could continue for forever. We believe the bad stuff, even if we are not aware of it. But how could that be? It means that our unconscious mind is at play here.

There is good news, though. *I am here to help you with your transformation, a spiritual makeover that will last you for forever.*

THE MIGHTY UNCONSCIOUS MIND

Some people may think that the unconscious, versus subconscious, versus conscious mind is hippie-dippy. However, anything that we fail to reject about ourselves consciously, we subconsciously accept about ourselves.

Stanford University psychiatrist and professor, Hans Steiner, explores the science of the motivational unconscious, in his continuing education program. Dr. Steiner says that *"all of us have unconscious processes that influence our behavior, perspective, interpretation of events, and emotional reactions."* He describes the three levels of our brain as the conscious mind (aware of sensory reactions to sound, vision, etc.), the motivational unconscious (mental activity underneath our consciousness that generally operates outside of our awareness but can be accessible), and our non-conscious mentation (e.g., mental processes, like neuronal activity such as breathing).[18]

People often read self-help books, attend workshops, and have endless goals and to-do lists, where managing them is unattainable.

---

18 https://scopeblog.stanford.edu/2012/05/07/your-secret-mind-a-stanford-psychiatrist-discusses-tapping-the-motivational-unconscious/

By continually planning for tomorrow, and living in the future, or reflecting on your mistakes of the past to avoid repeating them, you are rarely in the present moment.

You listen to motivational speakers for the *rah-rah*, in hopes that they will say something— anything—to put a fire in your belly to take serious action. You read articles online, and share them with your colleagues in hopes that you will motivate each other to make changes. You join book clubs and social clubs to be accepted and to avoid your feelings of failure and loneliness. And, if you are like most people, you wake up, go to a job that you dislike (or despise), and struggle in rush hour traffic to reach home to "loved ones" who show you no love. Ugh. That sounds awful! Is that really how you want to continue living?

I am here to tell you two things. One, you are not alone. And two, this can change.

If what you have read so far hasn't entirely freaked you out to the point that you decide to self-medicate, I encourage you to take a few deep breaths, and know that I have experienced incredible success with clients who were just like YOU. They had physical and mental health issues manifesting in their lives, which they were able to break through, and make life-long positive changes.

The truth is that intention is far more powerful than the will; that's precisely true, because your intentions will always come true. That is why, no matter how much hoping, wishing, or willing yourself to change, the result ends up being the same each time.

Many people go to their death, feeling unsatisfied or unfulfilled. They never achieved what their heart desired. Self-help gurus, and even mainstream media, now tell us that we are manifestation machines. You ask, and you shall receive. The Law of Attraction will enable you to get everything you desire—right? If you don't achieve your goals, what, or whom, is to blame?

Self-help guru and best-selling author, Dr. Wayne Dyer, in his book, *Power of Intention,* writes that *"The law of attraction is this: You don't attract what you want. You attract what you are."* The best-selling book by Rhonda Byrne, *The Secret,* sold 30 million copies worldwide, and her earlier video of the same name was a massive success. The experts featured in her book and video taught that the Law of Attraction could help people to manifest their goals in life by thinking of them.

Remember, the buck stops here. Only you can make real and lasting change in your life. I promise, if you join me on this journey, I will help you to learn how you can repair or correct any issues, struggles, or challenges that you are currently experiencing in your life.

So, what have we learned? You're fu*ked. Perhaps, but you don't have to be. You are, after all, exactly where you wanted or intended to be, according to your unconscious mind. Your conscious mind is saying that you need a severe mental makeover so that you can stop being hijacked by your unconscious mind!

"Sometimes I feel as if I'm wearing a divided, split brain in terms of drama and humor."

– Ridley Scott

THE DIVIDED BRAIN

Iain McGilchrist, the author of the acclaimed book, *The Master and His Emissary: The Divided Brain and the Making of the Western World*, has taken early research on the brain to a deeper and more profound level. McGilchrist says there is more unknown than known, about the brain, as every individual cell in our brain is a *"quite extraordinarily complex self-regulating and self-repairing system entirely unlike any wire that ever existed."*

With a billion neurons involved, and a reciprocal system, the number of connections in our brain are infinite. McGilchrist also challenges mainstream beliefs of the left versus right brain. *"Contrary to popular belief, it is the right hemisphere's, not the left hemisphere's, thinking that is more accurate, more down to earth—in a word, 'truer' to what is."* [19]

McGilchrist goes on to say how odd it is that the scientific community has, for the most part, *"ignored two absolutely fundamental and incontrovertible findings about the brain. First, that it is, literally,*

19 https://www.thersa.org/globalassets/pdfs/blogs/rsa-divided-brain-divided-world.pdf

profoundly divided. And second, its obvious asymmetry: there are clear observable differences at every level."

Historically, we thought of the brain as a machine, with each hemisphere performing a different role. However, McGilchrist says that both hemispheres perform the same functions, but they perform them differently, from a different viewpoint. *"For each hemisphere has a quite consistent, but radically different, 'take' on the world, which means that at the core of our thinking about ourselves, the world, and our relationship with it, there are two incompatible but necessary views that we need to try to combine. And things go badly wrong when we do not."*[20]

Why should you care about the brain hemispheres or different parts of the brain? Combining two contradictory but necessary views of ourselves, which McGilchrist introduces, is fundamental to my coaching work, and is central to my understanding of how I overcame my obstacles and challenges in life, and was able to share it with others.

So, while this highly scientific language can be difficult for most people to comprehend, please know that I have your back, and I will walk you through everything in this book so that you can apply the techniques that I'm offering to you, for your own life.

---

20 https://www.thersa.org/globalassets/pdfs/blogs/rsa-divided-brain-divided-world.pdf

BE CAREFUL WHAT YOU WISH FOR

Another one of my clients, Joe, came to me for help. At first glance, his predicament was confusing, as he was wealthy, attractive, and had women lined up around the corner to be with him! Why would Joe need my help? He achieved massive success in life. But—and this is a big but—he had cancer.

What's interesting is that Joe internalized the belief that "if something is too good to be true, it is too good to be true." He went through life with this core belief. He had all of the money that he ever needed, and he could retire at age 50. Many women desired him, making him the envy of other men. Through his belief that his incredible life was too good to be true, his unconscious mind internalized this message. So, when he was diagnosed with cancer, he was not surprised. The irony is that he created a disease to fit his reality. I will repeat: Joe created a disease in his body, to match his unconscious mind's truth ("My life is too good to be true."). I will share more about the work we did together, and Joe's results, in the following pages.

Joe's internalization of a limited belief, and saying it aloud, reminds me of my father. My father was healthy, as he came from a long line of strong men with good genetics. Case in point, his father, my grandfather, lived to be almost 100 years old. However, the last few years of my grandfather's life were quite painful to witness. My grandfather, a formerly strong, independent man full of vigor, suffered health problems that had him deteriorate into a man that was weak, needy, and reliant on others.

To become a helpless bystander, during my grandfather's metamorphosis from healthy to sick, caused my father to become disheartened; so much so, that he decided at that moment that he did not want to be weak or needy like his father. Therefore, my father started to say to himself, and aloud, that he *"would rather live to 60 years of age and be healthy, and one day just drop dead, than to suffer a long, painful death."*

I'm sure we have all heard the idiom, "Be careful what you wish for." My father should have heeded that advice.

.

2

Who Am I and What Will This Book Give You?

"It is not the most intellectual of the species that survives; it is not the strongest that survives; but the species that survives is the one that is able to adapt to and to adjust best to the changing environment in which it finds itself."

– Charles Darwin

In the previous chapter, I told you of my father's desire to live healthy to age 60 years and then pass on suddenly, versus living a long life that would likely involve a painful, chronic disease or illness that would have a long drawn out outcome. Well, it does not surprise me that my father lived for almost 60 years. Just three short months before his 60th birthday, he was diagnosed with cancer. My father was dead 15 days later.

I repeat, be careful what you wish for, as our unconscious mind is paying attention.

In this chapter, I want to briefly outline how I can help you to achieve extraordinary results. You will hopefully learn why I am the person, and that this is the time, to deliver information to you that can help you to transform your life.

I am a human being, just like you. I had a tough childhood, and as an adult, I experienced failures—just like you. However, today, I'm recognized as an international author, speaker, and coach, dedicating my life to helping others become their best selves.

NEW IMMIGRANT TO SUCCESS STORY

In 1986, I arrived in Canada with very little money. I spent six months in Vancouver, and on March 14, 1987, I moved to Toronto, with no more than $750 in my pocket. I had some obstacles to overcome, as I didn't know a soul and I spoke very little English.

However, I was determined to become my own boss because I did not want to work for anyone.

I remember that Toronto suffered one of the worst storms in its history that year. I had never experienced snow like this. I didn't even have the proper clothes. Despite my limited English skills, I met Maury Karakashian, a man with a beautiful soul, who invited me for a cup of coffee. He told me that $750 would not be enough to start a business, and he insisted that I should look for employment immediately. He warned me that I would end up living on the street, as Toronto rentals were expensive due to a massive housing shortage. Maury helped me by letting me use his phone. He was my main contact person, taking messages for me. I went to his place every evening to get my messages so that I could return calls for potential business opportunities.

Maury was a blessed man and a fantastic influence on me. Within three years, I was able to afford my own home. I also bought myself a large Mercedes. Once, I parked it in front of his shop, and then went inside to speak with him. He said, "Who is blocking the entrance to my shop?" I still remember the look on his face when he realized that I owned the fancy car! He was overjoyed, and hugged me as he said: "I hope you are not doing anything illegal!"

I later met, fell in love, and married my first wife in 1991. My children soon followed. After my daughter was born, I became very hungry for success. I opened a store that sold rugs. Driven for further success, I grew the company to an e-commerce (online) business, and at some point, we were shipping rugs to 40 different countries! I later sold my rugman.com business.

Next, I started a career as a business consultant, as I wanted to use my expertise to help other people build their own business. My consultation services later evolved into that of a coaching business, as I found that clients often had business and personal issues that required my help. Through word of mouth referrals, my coaching business grew. As a result, some of my coaching clients continue to come from far away to work with me, because they feel that I am the only one that can help them.

But why me? I was a child that grew up poor and was surrounded by conflict and war, who immigrated to Canada, and who Started in Rug business, and later sold a rug business. Why am I sought out by so many people?

It's because I took my business success and personal development results (for myself and my family), and transitioned it into a successful coaching business that impacts my clients mechanically, emotionally, and intellectually. I learned about human psychology and the human mindset, and applied it to my coaching. In a sense, I am a bit of a unicorn.

"Be a unicorn in a field of horses."

– **Unknown**

HUMBLE BEGINNINGS

But I have not always experienced a great life. My childhood was tough. I started from the ghettos of Tehran. I was born and raised in an impoverished area, which had its challenges. And I had to share the attention of my parents when my younger brother came along. Born premature, at only 4 pounds, my brother required more care and attention, as he was understandably frail.

Their lack of attention paid to me made me feel as if they did not care for me. I felt like I did not belong, and that I was not even loved. These feelings of being unlovable and unwanted followed me through my adolescence. As a child, I could relate to the main characters in the movies, *The Adventures of Huckleberry Finn* and *The Adventures of Tom Sawyer*.

I dreamed of going to university to become an engineer, but then the war began in Iran. The eight-year conflict began in September 1980, following Iraq's full-scale invasion of my country.[21] I was already growing up in poverty, amid the **Iranian Revolution, otherwise known as the Islamic Revolution (from 1978–77).**

Approximately 75% of the Iranian Army soldiers were dismissed because of the military Coup and this is exactly when Iraq invaded and a 8 year war began. Most soldiers came back dead or injured.

---

21 https://www.economist.com/newsbook/2012/06/21/what-happened

When I decided to join the Iranian Army, even they did not want me either, as I had flat feet and poor eyesight. I felt like it was just all downhill from there, and I desperately wanted to get out and make something of my life. After all of the killing and strife, I chose to leave my country for a better life.

MY RESET

Even with all of my business success, on my 40th birthday, I felt there was something wrong. Like with many other men, I found myself amid a midlife crisis. Or, perhaps it was an identity crisis. All I knew was that despite being financially successful, I felt empty inside. I felt hurt. My wife and I started to go to couples counseling. However, after three years of therapy, I was feeling far worse. I felt like nothing was going right with anything in my life. I went down the rabbit hole; I was embarking on a painful journey that was entirely new for me.

Going to therapy, and working through my issues, brought back painful memories and feelings of unworthiness. I felt depressed and anxious, and couldn't help feeling like I had just made the biggest mistake of my life. My depression worsened, and I experienced suicidal thoughts. The dark feelings and thoughts I was dealing with were complicated, creating chaos in my life. I couldn't help but feel like I completely screwed up by choosing to go to therapy. The troubles with my marriage, along with other issues that I was dealing with at the time, became even more prominent, as we attempted to work through our problems with a therapist.

A close family member also had a mental illness. So, with the problems that we were both facing, I decided that I would find a new way. I was determined to come out of this depression myself. I was going to stop the anxiety that plagued my brain and affected my decision-making abilities daily. And, I was also going to help my family member with their struggles.

So, naturally, I did the thing that most people wouldn't do—I stopped going to therapy! Instead, I embarked on a long, extensive, and expensive journey of healing. It was my vision quest but with a scientific spin to it.

From country to country, and guru to guru, I learned. On a quest to find what REALLY WORKS, I learned that I could actually help myself. The knowledge that I acquired during this time was mammoth. It shifted the ground beneath me. It woke me to my core.

With my newfound awareness and enlightenment, I was able to take what I learned to help my family member overcome their mental health challenges as well. The quality of life improved quite a bit, which sparked the idea that I could use what I learned to help others. That was the beginning of my coaching career.

I have dedicated my life to help anybody who wants to transform. I want to help people learn how to short circuit the complicated problems of moving past their trauma and life experiences to become successful. Throughout the years, I found the secret that makes things tick. I came to the country with nothing, and made something of my life. If I can do it, a poor boy from Tehran, then so could you!

Today, no issue scares me. I have conquered my fears in life, which has been liberating. This freedom allows me to be my best self. I want the same for the people who choose to work with me. I feel a sense of pride that I have been able to impart my knowledge and success onto my clients. One of my coaching clients told me that he made a million dollars after eight months of intensive work with me. Another client made a quarter-million dollars in his very first year in business.

Clients with emotional problems or depression have found relief. They have been able to move on with their lives to pursue their dreams and goals. Despite all of the success that I have helped my clients achieve, I am not a magician. I am a person who overcame these challenges and healed myself. I am proof that these techniques and theories work.

When people experience mental illness or emotional problems, underneath all of that pain is a person wanting to grow and heal. Something is not allowing them. No matter the trigger or issue that brought them to me, my clients had a sense of gratitude, because if they never experienced the original problem, they wouldn't have sought my help.

Human beings grow from a level of consciousness—from another level to another level. When you feel ready to grow, and you think you can do better in life, you do. It is incredible how one's mental health impacts business results. But of course, it does! As a higher level of consciousness arises, it becomes easier to make money, because people don't get caught into the mental games of scarcity and lack of abundance.

> *"You can't go back and change the beginning, but you can start where you are and change the ending."*
>
> – C.L. Lewis

WHY FOCUSING ON THE NEGATIVE STUFF DOESN'T WORK

I believe that therapy doesn't help us to move past our hurt. It may help us to understand our pain better, but it's difficult to separate what has happened in the past, and not allow it to overwhelm you to the point of it getting in the way of achieving positive results. The reason for this is because, as we talk about the negative stuff (e.g., painful past), we allow it to have a greater force and impact on our current life.

My wife and I invested an hour every week in therapy, hashing out our issues. We spent a crazy amount of money and had no visible results. Consequently, our relationship worsened; we both became depressed and ended up in divorce court, which is not a surprise since, in therapy, we are told to focus on developing relationships with ourselves.

How do you relate to yourself? Do you love yourself? Are you mean or harsh? Are you self-disciplining? Are you calm and relaxed? This type of inward self-discovery has become part of our culture. It has us all asking, "Who am I, and why am I the way I am?" We could spend years searching for these answers. But knowing this, will it gain you results in business? Will it help you become wealthy? It may help you relate to others better, and that's great. But most people looking for success want to change their wealth as well as their health. Therefore, asking yourself those questions will not help in this area. Instead, it will push you further from your goals.

If you are the type of person that believes you deserve to be successful, then congratulations—you and 99% of the population think the same thing. But the harsh reality is that only 1% of the population will become immensely wealthy and successful.

FINDING PEACE

I remember a long time ago that I thought about writing a book. But I thought, who am I to write a book? The voice in my head was difficult to ignore, as it asked, "Who do you think you are?" and "Who will ever read your book?"

These negative thoughts and self-doubts were typical of what I experienced before my reset. After all, it is not where you start in life but where you finish—right? I am a man who overcame obstacles and struggled with my success. I came to a place of peace and contentment.

Throughout my journey, I learned that the structure, or process, of healing, is more important than the "why" that psychologists and psychotherapists have us asking ourselves.

Asking ourselves why we do and say things is a death trap—getting caught up in the "why" is what destroyed my marriage. All of that talking with my wife had us unable to repair the mess we created. It was all such a waste of time. We were spinning around like a dog trying to chase its tail. We thought that by catching the tail, it would have the answers to our questions, and that life would be better—but the tail didn't matter! The act of spinning around, however, had an impact on our ability to move forward, as it was structural. It was part of the process, which I will elaborate on later.

When I am with a client, I am tuned into not only what they say but how they say it. Context, not content, is what provides me with insight into how I can best help them. And yet again, most therapies focus on the content of what has happened, and what is currently happening. Being bogged down with their woe-is-me story is not helpful, as it comes from a lower logical level, or lower level of consciousness. However, a higher level of consciousness is where real life-altering work begins.

When digging for answers, it is essential to know what you are looking for. What is stopping you from achieving success? What are your values? What are your beliefs? These are the vital questions to answer, as these types of mind patterns reveal your identity issues, and they provide me with a clear path to create effective, result-oriented therapy. I am a change agent that offers an intervention style of coaching.

Again, it's not necessary to understand why we are all screwed up, as most of us have overcome a challenge or trauma. What's important is how we internalized what happened into our core belief system.

At the beginning of my coaching career, I helped me and a family member to recover from mental illness. We are both successful and have found inner peace. I have helped my coaching clients achieve this peaceful state through their level of higher consciousness. That is the beauty in doing this type of work. The problems and issues of yesterday become today's opportunity to reset and recover. Together, we clean the road and pave the way for the client to truly flourish in their life.

MY LIFETIME DEDICATION

The client who once felt unsettled now feels ready for the next step of understanding and healing. They no longer want to make themselves busy, dealing with their past trauma, or their current life drama, with all kinds of things to keep them active and distracted. Distractions, such as smoking, boozing, gambling, drugging, shopping, etc., all stop us from growing.

However, when we decide that we are tired of all of the noise, we find ourselves at a new place of equilibrium. Evaluating where we are in our lives, and where we want to be, is the beginning of helping us to figure out our road map. With new growth, we can overcome any emotional, mental, or physical health issues. Our issues disappear.

Through the work, my clients gain new levels of consciousness that they are ready to explore and grow into. Once fearful and scared, they can raise the vibration and their level of consciousness. Their ego is no longer able to lie to them, telling them that they are not good enough, lovable enough, or worthy enough. They can fix areas in their lives because of the new peaceful state that they are in.

Tackling their marriage, money, or career problems no longer seems daunting to them. The results are incredible. But again, it is not magic or a miracle. **You will learn to work in harmony with the powerful forces that can open up a new world of opportunity for you!**

I know that my method works, as I have seen the results that my clients have achieved. I often hear myself say that I would give my right hand to have known this stuff when I was in my 30s! I wouldn't have suffered through depression, painful and useless marriage counseling, and divorce. My life would be very different.

"Investing in yourself is the best investment you will ever make. It will not only improve your life, it will improve the lives of all those around you."

– **Robin Sharma**

WHAT THIS BOOK IS AND WHAT I WILL BE GIVING YOU

What this book is not about:

- This book is not magic.

- This book is not mystical.

- This book is not about miracles.

- This book is not about delivering quick fixes.

- This book is not about your higher power.

MY PROMISE TO YOU AND YOUR INVESTMENT IN YOURSELF

I am about to describe my promise to you. But first I want a commitment from YOU.

Why do self-help gurus ask you to invest in yourself when they are selling you a program? Because the investment is not only monetary—it is a commitment. It's an undertaking that will consume your time, your mental and emotional energy, your creativity, and most importantly, your courage to be honest with yourself.

However, in return, you will experience invaluable returns on your investment. You will ignite your passion, desires, and goals, like you could never have imagined. If you are doing it right, your investment will be exhausting and invigorating at the same time. You will undoubtedly feel alive—truly alive.

You will discover, or re-discover, your purpose in life. You will fall in love with yourself all over again—or perhaps for the first time. You will know, and honestly believe, that you deserve greatness in your life.

All of this takes time and effort, which is why it is called an "investment." But all of this effort and investment is not for naught; it's with the hope and promise of achieving something big in the end. So, whether your reward or your *something big* is wealth, health, relationship success, or inner peace, YOU CAN ACHIEVE THIS if you heed my advice.

Here is what to expect…

My promise to you is that I will not hold anything back. I will equip you with the tools you need to create a brand new life for yourself. You will, within short order, witness enormous improvements that will give you the incentive to continue to do the work.

You need to give yourself 30 days to read my book from front to back, follow some daily practices, and complete some exercises. Spend an hour each day for the first 30 days, and then 15 minutes after that.

In the following chapters, you will have some daily practices to perform that will help you to grow and change. There will also be some exercises that will help provide insight into where you are now, and where you want to go.

Do not skip chapters or jump ahead, as I have built each exercise in a specific order. By following the content as it is delivered to you, you will have an optimum learning experience.

WHAT HAPPENS IF YOU DO NOTHING?

Earlier in this chapter, I provided you with a handful of reasons why you should not read my book. I have also provided you with ample reasons to continue reading. The bottom line is that if you want to make substantive changes in your life, you should not only keep reading but make it a priority to follow my recommendations. Learn from me, and allow me to coach and guide you to a **redesigned and renewed you**. Let's call it the version "2.0 You!"

The founder of analytical psychology, Carl Jung, said, *"I am not what has happened to me; I am what I chose to become."*

I couldn't agree more. I chose to learn about my anxiety and depression, and my family member's mental illness, so that we could recover. It took me a serious investment in time and money to acquire the knowledge that I am willing to share with you. I am delivering to you, on a silver platter, the benefits of the wisdom that I have acquired, not to mention the years of experience with coaching clients and helping them to transform their lives.

Again, human beings always have a choice. Your choices may not be perfect, but one will always be better than another.

Have the courage to admit that not choosing to act is also a choice. Living a dull, stagnant existence is no way to live. Do you think you were put on this earth to merely exist? To stay stuck? To wake up each day with a heavy heart, and to go to bed later, feeling like a failure? It is sad. More importantly, it is a waste of the life and opportunities that have been given to you.

So, what I am asking of you is to want MORE from your life, and MORE from yourself. I am not asking for excellence. I am asking for an effort that will ultimately net you positive results, and an effort that will give you a life that will exalt you—a life that would inspire you to scream from a rooftop; a life where your inner peace and contentment would be contagious for those around you; a life where your joy would ooze from your pores, with each breath that you take.

If you still lack motivation or commitment, ask yourself what will happen to your life if you choose to do nothing, to say nothing, to change nothing. What would your life look like in six months, one year, five years, or twenty-five years, for that matter?

- Will you be in a failing relationship?
- Will you be overweight, or worse, obese?
- Will you be one of those people who rely on antidepressants to get through the day?
- Will you be poor and one major illness away from becoming homeless?

- Will you be addicted to drugs or alcohol to self-medicate the pain away?

If you choose to do nothing, this could be you; or you could be that lucky person that got away, but the chances are small. You have more control over your outcome with a life based on your choices.

Do you choose to be the wealthy 1%? Or will you be one of the remaining 99%? Will you live a life of purpose, gratitude, and greatness? Will you continue to live a life controlled by your subconscious? Choose the former, and I will provide you with a blueprint that will bring you a personal transformation that is incredibly powerful and effective—a transformation that I have seen work for my clients—a robust yet natural transformation that I want for you!

"An investment in your personal development is the best investment you can make."

— **Jim Rohn**

WHAT THIS BOOK WILL DELIVER

This book is about merely getting hold of what you already have in your arsenal and, ultimately, connecting to yourself. This book is about getting control of what is already there. It is about getting a hold of where you are now, and unfolding into your 2.0 version.

To build a road map for you, we start with where you are now. Knowing where you are, and where you want to go, we can adequately address your current situation, and remedy it with a new way of thinking and a new way of doing things.

The quantum physics way of thinking suggests that we are a holographic reflection of the universe. Whatever we see out there in the world, exists here. And whatever we change here, changes the entire universe.

One of the professors involved in a multi-country study between Canada, the UK, and Italy is researching that very thing. Professor Kostas Skenderis explains: *"Imagine that everything you see, feel, and hear in three dimensions (and your perception of time), emanates from a flat, two-dimensional field. The idea is similar to that of ordinary holograms, where a three-dimensional image is encoded in a two-dimensional surface, such as in the hologram on a credit card. However, this time, the entire universe is encoded!"*[22]

Some people believe that the greater universe has to change in order for them to see changes in their own life. But the change does not have to come from another source. People who wait for change to come from external sources to heal or fix themselves will not get results.

---

22 https://www.southampton.ac.uk/news/2017/01/holographic-universe.page

Every person has the same ability to heal themselves, as they share the same mechanics— neurology, physiology, and cells are all common between every single human being. Furthermore, I believe that everyone has a talent. I don't think that some people are smarter or dumber than others. Where the difference lies is with how they are measured.

For example, while one person may score higher on IQ (intelligence quotient) tests, another may have higher EQ (emotional intelligence). Or they may have killer survival instincts. Rhodes scholar versus a bushman—they are the same. However, we evaluate them from different perspectives. The same applies to people of different races, cultures, religions, or genders. They all share the same humanness (e.g., the mechanics) but may shine in their perspective areas. As humans, wouldn't it be wonderful if we all embraced and celebrated these differences?

IF ONLY I KNEW IN MY 20'S WHAT I KNOW NOW...

Looking back on my life, I can't help but think of how different things would be if I knew in my twenties what I know now. Because I assuredly understand that this knowledge is priceless, I would have done anything back then to attain it. I would have given my right arm!

If I had access to this information when I was 20 years old, I would have lived a very different life. I would have been a completely different person as a result. I would not have endured certain hardships that I experienced. However, if I hadn't taken the hard, difficult road, I would not have discovered the massive learning that has transformed my life.

Like many people, I went through painful heartbreaks and a devastating breakdown of a marriage. Sadly, I also suffered from debilitating depression. I can relate to my clients, which makes me unique. I am not one dimensional.

I call myself a unicorn because my valuable and diverse experience is unusual, rare, and unique. I have a strong business background that has earned me into the eight figures. On the flip side of that, I experienced terrible business hardship, and had to learn to fight my way back. All of this experience is exceptional to find in a coach.

People go through challenges, and overcome these challenges. It's what makes us human. The ability to love and feel, to know pain and sorrow, and to forgive and forget are experiences that we can all relate to.

You, my friend, are on the cusp of discovering your greatness. You will be able to see the essence of my knowledge, as I am about to share my journey and lessons with you. You are at a turning point in your life.

YOU ALWAYS GET YOUR INTENTIONS FULFILLED, BUT YOU DON'T ALWAYS GET WHAT YOU WANT

Who is calling the shots in your life? Do your words and thoughts honestly have the power to affect your present and to direct your future?

In 1956, cognitive psychologist, George A. Miller, of Harvard University's Department of Psychology, conducted a study: *The Magical Number Seven, Plus or Minus Two: Some Limits on Our Capacity for Processing Information*. What his study found was that most adults can store between five and nine items in their short-term memory, and that the average, or "magic," number was seven.[23]

Why this study is essential is that it explains our ability to process or retain information consciously at one time. If we believe in the logic behind the dual brain system, then we should expect to get in life what we want, plus or minus two.

A standard deviation of one or two is possible, but stretching a standard deviation to three, doesn't happen. So, what we expect and what we deserve are also impacted by this standard deviation of one or two.

---

23 https://elearningindustry.com/magical-number-seven-plus-
    minus-two-memory-affects-the-perception-of-information

Do you have things happen that surprise or shock you? Say, for example, if you wake up one day to find that you let your marriage or your business fail. You may tell your friends that you did not want it to fail, but that is your consciousness speaking.

Unbeknownst to you, there is a part of yourself that said the words (that you wanted to fail). How do you know this? Because your unconscious mind is calling the shots, and it's getting its *Intel* from what you consciously and unconsciously say to yourself.

Your unconscious mind is the master of your consciousness— just like a puppet in a puppet show. It pulls your strings, but it is kind enough to remain in the background so that you think you have done this consciously.

People think that they are in control; but it's like putting a child behind the wheel of a car that is being controlled by artificial intelligence (A.I.). The child might be thrilled, thinking that he's driving the car. As in this example, where the child is not in control, the unconscious mind is the more significant Intel source inside of us; and it guides everything you have in your life, such as hardship, breakups, and even physical diseases.

There is a reason you sometimes feel like a victim in your life— it is because you have been. But don't go too far to look for the perpetrator!

But I'm here to tell you that it does not have to be that way. You can become enlightened and gain real control for the very first time in your life!

The self-help industry says that if you want something, you can have it by manifesting it. The truth is that what you are living now is all of your manifestations that you may not be consciously aware of. However, there is a significant disconnect between the conscious mind and the unconscious mind.

The logical type of thinking that goes in the unconscious mind is vastly different from the logical kind of thinking that goes into the conscious mind. These two forces that drive our thoughts make us the most exciting and diverse beings on earth.

However, if we can learn to coordinate and work both of them, this synergy is what facilitates humans to create beautiful poetry, to succeed in business, and to flourish in love.

All that happens the minute you go to one side or the other. However, if you venture too much or too far, you will ignore the other side completely. This book will teach you how to be in integrity with yourself by communicating back and forth with your unconscious mind, and you will gain an understanding of the intentions, wants, needs, and desires of the unconscious mind. You already know what the wants, needs, and desires are of the conscious mind so that you can exchange the information with the unconscious mind to get support and buy-in. You will learn to optimize the resources of both the conscious mind and the unconscious mind.

Some people are so fearful of their unconscious mind that they don't trust it. However, the unconscious mind is the one that can be relied on. Imagine if you relied on your conscious mind to beat your heart and digest food, or to perform many of the millions of tasks that are being done within us daily without fail and without our awareness. Your conscious mind could not handle it. But lucky for us, our unconscious mind is powerful and can take care of everything that needs to get done for us to live and thrive as human beings!

3
How It All Began

"The real question is not whether machines think but whether men do. The mystery which surrounds a thinking machine, already surrounds a thinking man."

– B. F. Skinner

HOW DID THIS ALL BEGIN?

In other words, how did we all become so fu*ked? This chapter will explain how we are handed down a set of beliefs, values, and programs, which impact every thought, behavior, and action we have taken since we were children.

THE BLACK BOX

The black box is pure conditioning from our parents. As an infant, the love flowed from our parents to us freely. There were no limits to the love that they bestowed upon us during this time in our life, as our hearts were open and pure. However, somewhere between the age of two and four, our parents began to tame us. They conditioned us based on how we behaved, and they started to withdraw love from us when we did things that did not meet their approval.

By withholding love from us, our parents instilled in us their set of values, beliefs, and manners. This tool of withdrawing love to condition our children was devised by society many, many years ago, to bring up people who could live in harmony with everybody else.

Think about it; if there was nobody else in our society, you could do what you wanted. You would have no one telling you what to think, say, or do. And, based on your actions, you would receive no feedback or stimuli from them. As a result, many of your beliefs and values would not exist.

Also because the attention we get when we are sick or hurt and Fail we learn to be a victim and look for attention by becoming sick and fail in adulthood.

What is shocking to come to terms with is that others form your beliefs. You did not choose them. You were coerced into becoming a certain way, and if you were not what was expected, then you were shunned and considered immoral.

Because this type of conditioning makes us into a mirror image of our parents, it does not allow us to be the loving beings that we genuinely are. It does not allow us to experience life in the present moment.

As a professor of psychology at Harvard University, B.F. Skinner developed The Black Box Theory of Behaviorism. Skinner's theory was "based upon the idea that learning is a function of change in overt behavior. Changes in behavior are the result of an individual's response to events (stimuli) that occur in the environment."[24] Skinner believed that the important thing was to "understand the relationships between the input (stimulus) and output (response) through the 'black box.'"

As children, we have preconceived notions about what things mean. We ask ourselves, "Is it good?" "Is it bad?" "Do they approve or

---

24 https://www.instructionaldesign.org/theories/operant-condi tioning/

disapprove?" We become obsessed with appeasing others—especially our parents.

As children, we create a false sense of self because we do not have the supports in place to become independent of our parents. This false self is how it sounds: It is a fake persona that we create as children to protect ourselves from experiencing distress in our close relationships, and from re-experiencing trauma and shock. When we are our false self or public self, we are polite, well-mannered, and everything our parents and society told us to be.[25]

But sadly, we are NOT our true selves. As a result of this conditioning, and living an inauthentic life, we end up going through life unconsciously, unaware of the things that make us feel, think, and react.

As human beings, we are dynamic. However, a part of us, our ego, becomes frozen or static. All of the firm beliefs that we have formed around our life—around wealth, around money, around relationships—question who we are and what we can or cannot do. These are all part of the ego.

Bestselling author, Deepak Chopra, says that *"The ego, however, is not who you are. The ego is your self-image; it is your social mask; it is the*

---

25 https://weinholds.org/how-the-false-self-gets-created/

role you are playing. Your social mask thrives on approval. It wants control, and it is sustained by power because it lives in fear."[26]

To get to the route of the black box, the identity, and the ego, when I first see a client, I have them write out lists of 20 responses to the following questions: "Who am I?" "I can…," "I cannot…." All of these examples are important, as many of these will reveal their truths. More importantly, their ugly truths will reveal themselves as the saboteur parts of themselves.

I also ask my clients to complete some handouts with over 300 questions, which help to reveal what is happening inside of them, of which they are not aware. These essential answers illustrate things such as why you behave a certain way, or why you like certain things or like certain people.

But because these are all part of your black box, there is engineering (structure) to it. Therefore, with a change to the smallest component, you will create a shift, which can bring hope that evolving the social conditioning and behavior is possible.

You cannot change a prominent structure, but you can change a small component of a prominent structure. To achieve this end, you have to go to the minor part of your black box, which stores your beliefs and values.

---

26 https://www.goodreads.com/work/quotes/822128-the-seven-spiritual-laws-of-success-a-practical-guide-to-the-fulfillmen

"Most people are other people. Their thoughts are someone else's opinions, their lives a mimicry, their passions a quotation."

– Oscar Wilde

FORMING IDENTITY AND BELIEFS

Human beings within our society have become such victims that they are building tribes to have protection in numbers. Just look at the *tribal* identity politics that exist within the USA today, since Donald Trump won the presidency.

You cannot solve a problem at the level where the problem lies. Instead, it has to be addressed at a higher level. Once you know where the problem lies, you need to go to the smallest component and change it. Your beliefs are the component of this identity. When you change the elements, the identity will shift, and the ideal world will exist for you.

Most people are living very differently from their ideal world because it is difficult to achieve this level. I have seen enlightened people who have stopped believing in the process. I helped them to eliminate most of their negative beliefs, and I helped them to clear out the *junk messages* so that they could be open, and move toward their ideal world. Once in that place, it is like seeing for the very first time in your ideal world. Everything is now exciting and new, as you would have no memories of the past affecting your view.

But the ideal world is not necessarily for everyone. You can have a belief that is causing you to act in specific ways. Let's use one of my coaching clients as an example. He is the one who had everything, but he was dying from cancer. He had this belief that if something was too good to be true, it was not going to work. I worked with him on two different fronts. I wanted to know where he got his belief that if it is too good to be true, then it would fail or something disastrous would happen. He also believed that if something good happened, something terrible was going to happen afterward to balance it out.

The important thing, when working with limiting beliefs, was to find out what the core beliefs were. The next step was to dig behind the limiting beliefs to find the smallest structure, which created a miniature shift. A shift like this is similar to turning the lights on in an entire city, all at once. Turn the main switch on the brain, and it lights up the whole part of the brain that was dark.

The black box is what is inside of us. We are not aware of the internal dialogue, the identity, and the beliefs forming, as they are out of our control because we were pushed into this identity.

An unfixed, or fluid, identity creates uncertainty and unsafety for others because people often want to put you in a box. When you cannot be put into a box or labeled, it makes others feel unsafe or uncomfortable. Therefore, we tend to put others in boxes to force them to conform to our standards.

Marketing companies have found this secret, and today, they are using this type of psychology to make everything a brand. Why? They know that brands sell. Brands become popular and successful because consumers are confident that they will always get what they expected, meaning that they will get whatever the brand or product promised them. Therefore, people are often willing to pay more for brand-named merchandise.

Similarly, people look for an identity in another human being, just as they would a product. When you look for an identity in a human being, he/she has to tell you who they are for you to feel safe. Then you have to differentiate one from the other, which is done in our heads without being consciously aware of it happening.

"Meditation is the dissolution of thoughts in eternal awareness or pure consciousness without objectification, knowing without thinking, merging finitude in infinity."

– Voltaire

THINKING VERSUS REMEMBERING

Most people very seldom think. Instead, people often use their memory to solve problems. I remember one time when I was at my rug store in Montreal. A very nice Jewish gentleman came in. He wanted to trade in an expensive watch that was once owned by his grandfather, in exchange for a rug. He no longer wanted the Swiss

Patek Philippe watch because it brought back painful memories of his grandfather, who was a Holocaust survivor.

I tried on the wristwatch to see how it felt. The watch looked great. When I wanted to take it off, I couldn't do it. It would not allow me to open the latch. The grandson also did not know how to take it off.

I found myself getting a bit pissed off because I did not want to pick up the energy of a man who was tormented in Nazi Jewish concentration camps. I was concerned that I would have nightmares.

If it were a cheap watch, I would have used pliers to remove it. But, due to the delicacy, I took it to a jeweler that I knew. The jeweler took a moment to look at it, and he placed a finger on the watch, and it opened up! He explained that the latch on these watches was on the other side as that of regular watches.

Out of habit, I kept trying to open it the same way over and over again. That was my memory taking control, trying to open the watch unsuccessfully.

Another example of people not thinking is if you take the hinges off a door and put them on the other side—adults can become confused, stuck, and unable to open the door. However, a young child in the same scenario would be able to figure it out quickly, because they have not been through the same level of conditioning as adults. It has not yet been mentally beaten into them.

Adults stop thinking. Instead, they use their memory to get through life. This entire process of memorization gets reinforced in schools. Teachers do not teach us how to think; teachers show us how to remember. This type of brainlessness is the reason why so many people are poor, why less than 1% of the population is super-wealthy, and only 10% of people in the Western hemisphere is well to do. We do not learn to think for ourselves, nor do we learn to be present. We are required only to remember.

But why would education institutions teach us to be brainless idiots? Industrialists, at the turn of the century, did not want competitors. They wanted good followers. Therefore, the educational system was an intentional design that caused us to all become a product of the Industrial Revolution. Schooling became standardized. It also became a trap that has held us down.

Think about it. Look at some of the wealthiest people in the world, like Steve Jobs. Jobs is worth $54 billion. He didn't do well at Stanford University because he was an individual thinker, which went against what schools were teaching.

I like to tell people that I have an MBA (Millionaire by Accident), because I did not go to university.

Again, when you are not remembering, you are thinking, and you are present, making it easier to solve problems much faster, which means that for us to unfu*k our lives, or to get out of our current predicaments, we need to be present instead of dealing with our memory to get through life.

Do you remember your dreams? Are you a pirate or an adventurer? Are you the same gender? Are you another person?

We are like a white piece of paper. Whatever you write goes into a file in your mind. For example, I have seen hypnotists put people into a deep trance through hypnosis, and tell them that they are not who they think they are. The file says your name. So, when asked, your mind immediately goes there and looks for your name. You search into your memory and are confident of the answer. But this is remembering—it is not thinking. If a hypnotist tells a person that their name is something different, when hypnotized, the person will not be able to recall their name. Instead, they will relay the name that was provided by the hypnotist. I have seen this performed many times.

> *"The unconscious mind of a man sees correctly even when conscious reason is blind and impotent."*
>
> – **Carl Jung**

CONSCIOUS AND THE UNCONSCIOUS MIND

The conscious mind is a very new thing. The Unconscious mind, or the Unconscious awareness, is part of our automated sympathetic nervous system. When you are speaking with someone, the words you choose to use means you are conscious, or aware, of the conversation. But our unconscious mind does the bigger job like assembling the words and creating sentences.

We had an unconscious mind way before our conscious mind was even developed. The power of the unconscious mind is shocking. Bruce Lipton has done an extensive study of the conscious versus unconscious mind, and he found that the unconscious mind is in control about 95% to 99% of the time, and our conscious mind is in control only 1% to 5% of the time. Dr. Lipton says that *"the unconscious mind operates at 40 million bits of data per second, whereas the conscious mind processes at only 40 bits per second. So, the unconscious mind is much more powerful than the conscious mind, and it is the unconscious mind which shapes how we live our life."*[27]

Did you get that? The unconscious mind processes 40 million bits of data per second, whereas the conscious mind processes only 40 bits of data per second.

There is a joke about the power of the unconscious mind that I want to share with you...

There was a man who climbed a high tree. When he reached the top, he began asking God for his help to get down. He said, "Oh, my

---

27 http://www.lifetrainings.com/Your-unconscious-mind-is-running-you-life.html

God, there's no freaking way I can get back down there. I will sacrifice my bull for you if you help me to climb down to the bottom." He climbs down a bit and says, "God, I changed my mind. Instead of the bull, I will sacrifice a sheep for you if you help me to get down to the bottom." The man proceeds to climb down further, and said: "Okay God, instead of the sheep, I will sacrifice a rooster for you, if you help me get down to the bottom."

The man continues to climb down the massive tree, and sees that he is close enough to the ground to jump. At this point, he says, "You know what God, I just lied. Everything I said to you was a lie. I just wanted to get down safely. I wasn't going to sacrifice anything for you." The man jumps off the tree and, unbeknownst to him, right underneath the tree, is an old, deep well. He fell through the well cover and to the bottom of the well. Bleeding and in pain, with broken bones from his injuries, the man says, "God, it looks like you don't take a joke very well."

The moral of this story is that you should not joke around with your unconscious mind. The man in the joke kept saying that he wanted to get to the bottom, and his unconscious mind delivered.

When dealing with the unconscious mind, you need to be honest and direct, and to say what you want. If you say what you don't want, you are going to get what you don't want. The unconscious mind does not hear the "don't" part, as it focuses on the main content, just as it did with the man's desire to get down to the bottom.

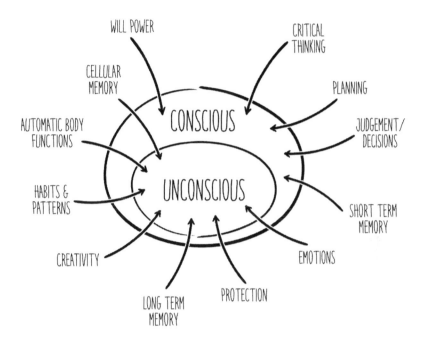

Figure 1. [28]

"*You are always in the process of creating. Every moment, every minute, every day. You are a big creation machine, and you are turning out a new manifestation literally as fast as you can think.*"

– **Neale Donald Walsch**

28 www.diyabodymind.com

THE CONSCIOUSNESS IS OUR MANIFESTATION MACHINE

The unconscious mind is a massive manifestation machine.

Imagine you have a Magic Genie, and the Genie asks you what you want. It is always at your service. For example, if you say that you DON'T want to be poor, then your unconscious mind will give you a lot of poor; or if you say that you DON'T want to be sick, your unconscious mind will make sure that you are very sick, because your unconscious mind then focuses on one thing: being poor or sick. It does not differentiate poor versus not poor.

Therefore, to deal with the unconsciousness, you need to be straight and positive. Instead of saying that you "like it when your glass is not half empty," say that you "like it when your glass is half full." Remember, your unconscious mind will hear the word, *empty,* and think that is what you want.

Examples of direct, positive messages:

- If WEALTH is what you want, focus on that. You would say, "I am wealthy" instead of "I am not poor."

- If HEALTH is what you want, focus on that. You would say, "I am healthy," instead of "I am not sick."

Again, DO NOT FOCUS ON WHAT YOU DO NOT WANT, or your manifestation machine (your unconscious mind) will deliver what you do not want!

My father is an excellent example of this, as he focused on the negative. He consistently said, "I want to live to 60 years but have a very healthy and happy life." And he died shortly after his 60th birthday. His manifestation machine delivered his wish to him: to be dead at age 60.

The unconscious mind is also very sneaky, as it is continuously listening to the critical conversations that we have in our heads. Whenever we are thinking of ideas, problem-solving, or conversing with others,; the unconscious mind is listening. Therefore, you have to be careful what you wish for others. You see, what you wish for others, the unconscious mind thinks that you want it for yourself. If you wish harm onto others, you will be the recipient of the harm.

I come from Iran, where the most significant thing they say is, "Down to America." They have chanted those words for decades. Consequently, Iran is a country that does not have its brand, politics, or international influence. All they have is a society that has been "downing" themselves for years.

We can all learn from Iran's lesson. It's arduous because other beliefs make you feel less than. That is why comparing yourself to others is such a big problem. Thinking or feeling less of yourself in comparison to someone else keeps you down. So stop doing it!

Best-selling author and spiritual messenger, Neale Donald Walsch, says that the power of creation is always turned on. Walsch says, *"The Energy of Attraction, you see, responds not only to what we desire but also to what we 'fear.' Not only to what we wish to draw to us, but also to what we wish to 'push away.' Not only to what we consciously choose, but also to what we 'unconsciously' select."*

That is why the best way to counter any negative feelings and fear that you may have is to count your blessings. **When you are focused on what is right in your life, and you experience genuine gratitude, you will feel amazing.** It is almost like a feeling of euphoria, as you become overwhelmed with feelings of extreme joy and happiness, and can experience an all-natural buzz, or a sense of being *high on life*. You will want to experience these intense, uplifting feelings some more, and your unconscious mind will know that you liked these things, and will give you more of them.

> *"If you want to find the secrets of the universe, think in terms of energy, frequency, and vibration."*
>
> **– Nikola Tesla**

VIBRATION AND ENERGY

What you think of, and how you feel, creates a vibration within your body, and it happens whether you are thinking of positive things about yourself or wishing bad things on others. The energy is a black box. The energy is the motion for the information. We call energy the information and the motion. So, if you go to the smallest component (the information), you will have full control.

When you break it down to the component of the information that exists within the energy, then you are onto something great, as it is a straightforward exchange.

For example, let's say that you are not happy because somebody else is doing better than you, and it upsets you. Instead of saying, "I want to be like that person; he/she is such a good role model," you are likely to complain about the other person and criticize them.

This negative messaging prompts your body chemistry to create changes. As human beings, we have neurotransmitters (chemical messengers) and neural inhibitors (that interrupt or block activity). Your inhibitors will inhibit you from achieving a self-induced state, and your state is crucial for helping you to achieve your goals in life.

I will break this down into simpler terms. Action produces certain results. But the state (i.e. mood) you are in, controls your actions. For example, if you are in a good mood (a positive state), you could go into a crappy situation and turn it around. However, if you are in a bad mood (a negative state), you could go into a good situation and turn it into a bad one.

We all have up (good) days and down (bad) days. So, how is the state determined? I'm glad you asked! Our physiology controls it, as our state is determined by our thoughts, our beliefs, our values, and what we say to ourselves. Our state controls the behavior output, or our actions, which allows us to go to the lowest level, which is where our beliefs lie. Once dissected, you will discover what is inhibiting you, shifting your identity, changing your state, and producing a different outcome.

One thing to remember about energy is that you need to be careful not to take on other people's energy. The alternative health industry promotes various types of *energy work* to balance the systems of energy throughout the body, to eliminate or alleviate symptoms of many illnesses. But I believe this work is hazardous, since you do not know what energy, sickness, or disease the other person has. Therefore, it is best to avoid these types of alternative therapies, such as Reiki.

> *"The key to growth is the introduction of higher dimensions of consciousness into our awareness."*
>
> – **Laozi**

AWARENESS

Anything that is outside of our conscious awareness is a part of our unconscious mind. An example of this is anything within our body. Our body functions without us actively having to provide it with commands when we perform certain activities, such as drinking water, opening a box, knocking on a door, or climbing a set of stairs.

However, you can bring attention to a part of your body, bringing awareness to your conscious mind. For example, your new shoes are causing a blister on your foot. You may not be mindful of how your feet manage to take steps when walking. However, your conscious mind becomes aware of the pain caused by the new blister forming on your heel.

You need to take that awareness and shift it. Say you point a flashlight towards a dot in front of you—wherever you focus the flashlight, is where your attention is, which is plus or minus two. The attention span of a conscious mind is competing against 40 million bits of information per second, which is the processing power of the unconscious mind.

It takes a lot for your unconscious mind to become overwhelmed. You have to work hard to overcome it. Therefore, it takes a lot of work to become neurotic! The conscious mind has a different way of communicating from that of the unconscious mind. Moreover, the logical levels of the unconscious mind and conscious mind are entirely different types.

We have no judgment in the unconscious mind, as everything there is pure. That is why, when you say, "I don't want this," you get it. Solely focusing on what you do not want, gets you the very thing you don't want! The pureness of the unconscious mind provides you with your wishes in their purest form.

The conscious mind, on the other hand, is aware. Your language falls into the domain of the unconscious mind. We are very rarely realistic. Either we are too scared, or we are too optimistic, or too pessimistic; but we are never really in the center.

The unconscious mind functions using its sensory systems. Whatever it senses, is present there, and these beliefs, once they become unconscious, become a domain of the unconscious mind. Then, the unconscious mind filters through to you, all the information that is going through it.

The unconscious mind is one big machine that likes to automate everything, which is why you don't learn anything unless you become unconsciously competent.

We aspire to become unconsciously competent because, at this level, we use our new skills effortlessly, performing tasks without any conscious effort. Some would call this level *mastery*. With the last level, when your unconscious mind is doing it for you, you will never forget. An example is when you learn to ride a bicycle at age ten. You will always remember the mechanics of riding, because your unconscious mind is doing this for you.

Four levels of learning – Conscious competence[29]

Unconscious Incompetence – We don't know what we don't know

Conscious Incompetence – We know what we don't know

Conscious Competence – We know what we know

Unconscious Competence – We don't know what we know

---

29 https://rapidbi.com/four-levels-of-learning/

When you become unconsciously competent, you can succeed, as your conscious mind lets you. Let's say that the conscious mind is not trusting your unconscious mind, and you won't let it go; you will not presume to perform at a certain level. So, it will take a lot longer to learn; whereas someone like Beethoven was a natural musician and composer, as he learned to trust himself. He allowed that pure being inside of himself to produce music that the whole world would fall in love with. His self-doubt was not present.

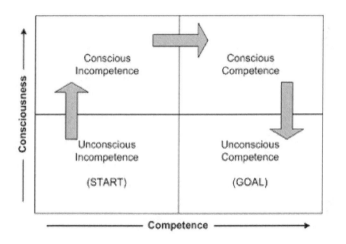

Figure 2.[30]

Awareness is what we learn through our five senses: sight (vision), sound (hearing), smell (olfaction), taste (gustation), and touch

30 https://examinedexistence.com/the-four-states-of-competence-explained/

(tactile perception). Our sensory-based system allows us to collect information from the world; then we process it in our brain, and we interpret what it means. The interpretation is *not* the awareness; instead, it is the interpretation *of* awareness.

For example, my perceptions or opinions of how someone else looks (e.g., tall vs. short, big vs. small, blonde vs. brunette), is not reality. These perceptions are my interpretation of how these people look.

We all have different ideas on what beauty or strength is. That is why my opinions, or perceptions of someone else, are just interpretations—because it differs from someone else's interpretation. You could say that these interpretations are similar to the saying that *beauty is in the eye of the beholder*, which means that it is the observers who determine what is, or is not, beautiful.

When your language becomes an accounting system, directly correlating items and then naming and transferring data for communication with other people, then that is close to reality. That's awareness. However, the minute you go into interpreting the awareness, by adding your values and judgments, your values and judgments are added to the data and announced to others as if it's true. But it's not true. For example, when you say, "a tall man," the word, *man*, is a reality (assuming he is truly a man). But "tall" is an interpretation that depends on how tall you are. If in comparison, you are 7 foot 4 inches, then the other man may not be tall to you. However, if you are only 4 foot 5 inches, then he is.

We often compare people for their differences, but these so-called differences are all subjective. Instead, our awareness is part of the accounting of what we see, hear, and feel. If you say, "I feel uncomfortable," it's an awareness of a translation. Uncomfortable is an interpretation of certain sensations. But if you say that you can feel a throbbing sensation in your chest, then that would be awareness.

You may think that saying that you "see a big car" is awareness, but it is a translation of particular awareness, because it is at the sensation level of awareness. Saying that you "see a car," is awareness, because you did not interpret the car's appearance, just the presence of it.

Awareness is where you feel warm. You see, hear, taste, feel, and smell certain things. But awareness is not emotion. If you say that you smell something disgusting, this comes from memory. So, awareness is a clear, intentional direction of our senses. What this means is that I see, feel, hear, smell, and taste without any interpretation attached to it.

That is pure awareness, and the rest is all memory. Once you go into your memory bank, it becomes like the example of the expensive watch that was stuck on my wrist for two days. All I had to do was put my thinking cap on, but I was stuck; I was trying to use my memory to solve the problem, instead of using my thoughts.

Most people have very little awareness. Mindfulness meditation is excellent, as it helps people to become present so that they can take inventory of their awareness. By focusing on their breath, they can hear their heartbeat, feel their feet touching the ground, clasp their hands that are placed on their lap, and feel the gentle touch of their skin.

Through meditation, you become centered and present. If you rotate through your inventory, three or four times, by saying to yourself, "I see this, I feel this, I taste this, I hear this," you will become present at the moment, and will then be able to start to think.

Awareness, without any interpretation or evaluation, is the only tool we have. Even rich people think they are poor, because they compare themselves to billionaires like Bill Gates. But this type of thinking creates a false perception. Real awareness will not give you that. Real awareness will provide you with an accurate data point that you can hang your hat on.

4

The Unseen World of the Unconscious Mind

"A *pill cannot make your unconscious, conscious.*"

– Serena Jade

WHAT IS THE UNCONSCIOUS MIND?

This chapter is going to be about the unconscious and conscious mind, and their differences. People often think that their conscious mind controls them, yet they have no idea that they are experiencing consciousness as an unconscious being.

You may have heard the saying that *we are spiritual beings living human lives*. This saying refers to our unconscious mind.

Our unconscious mind is colossal, as it is everything that is unbeknownst to us. Our unconscious mind is everything that is within our body and mind that occurs automatically. Driving a car is an example, where some of the driving, such as watching the roads, deciding on a route to take, or turning on your signal indicator, is all part of your conscious mind.

However, your ability to drive the car—using the gears, gas pedal, and brake pedal—is all part of your unconscious mind. You don't need to tell your foot to apply pressure to the brake. Your unconscious mind sends the signal to your foot for you. All of this messaging from your brain to your body parts occurs without your being aware, which means that your unconscious mind has mastered driving.

This type of behind-the-scenes activity is similar to when a violinist masters how to play his instrument. He consciously reads the music when playing. However, his ability to play the instrument so exquisitely has been mastered to the point that his unconscious mind does it for him. Sigmund Freud compared the human mind to an iceberg, with the small tip of the iceberg (that is visible to us) being the conscious mind, and the bulk of the iceberg (that is hidden from our view) being the unconscious mind.

We have no awareness of what or how our unconscious mind is processing information. Since the bandwidth for the conscious mind is only seven, plus or minus two, it is like we have only a bucket of water. Meanwhile, there is an ocean (the unconscious mind) that we cannot access. We can only get one bucket of water at a time. Since we are only aware of the bucket, we think that is all there is.

Therefore, if we want to experience some other part of the ocean, we would need to empty the bucket to sample the ocean water. Therefore, if you are going to become aware of your heart, you need to calm down and relax in order to get your conscious bandwidth to open for you so that you can tune into deeper parts of the unconscious mind.

However, sometimes, we can access some parts of us that are not conscious. For example, if I asked you about the temperature of your left toe, your attention would go to your left toe, and you would suddenly become aware of the temperature of your left toe, because you are accessing a part of your unconscious mind.

To access parts of our unconscious mind, we need to become very still and quiet. Paying close attention to our breath, we inhale and exhale, as we become aware of the sound and rhythm of our heartbeat. We will hear other sounds that were not available to us when we were not still. But as we quiet our mind and pay attention, we start to feel our heartbeat. The awareness of our internal systems, such as our heart beating, brings us closer to a connection with our unconscious mind. Scientists have proved that those who practice mindfulness meditation regularly are more aware of their unconscious mind, which gives them a sense of conscious control over their bodies.

Some people meditate to train their mind or induce a mode of consciousness. However, most people use meditation to focus or quiet their brain, to reach a higher level of awareness and inner calm. Similarly, people choose to use hypnosis as a useful tool to achieve an altered state of consciousness, as we can become aware of and communicative with certain parts of our unconscious mind when in this altered state.

Being in a hypnotic trance takes it to another level, as the depth of the trance can vary. Hypnosis has been used for centuries to heal the mind, body, and soul. Universities have started to study the efficacy of hypnosis with pain management, and they have found it to be superior to other active treatments. Moreover, Western medicine is becoming aware of the benefits of using hypnosis for their patients, as it assists with pre and post-surgery pain. There have also been cases of hypnosurgery, where a patient is sedated with only the use of hypnotherapy, instead of traditional <u>anesthetics</u>.

"The unconscious mind is anything that we are aware of internally but not conscious of."

– **Aslan Mirkalami**

We are not consciously aware of the internal processes that take place within our bodies. But when you become quiet, you will consciously hear what your unconscious mind hears all the time.

Inside the unconscious mind are millions of activities taking place simultaneously. Imagine you are in a dark room and no one is there; your consciousness is like a flashlight that lights up certain areas that you want to see.

Our unconscious mind is aware of a lot more than we are, internally or externally. It controls our internal functions, and it is mindful of subtleties such as another person's heartbeat, breathing pattern, pupils, or anything that might indicate if a person is upset or in distress, or if they are happy to see you. The unconscious mind is taking care of all of the subtle signals that the conscious mind does not consciously detect, even though we may get a feeling that something is out of place. Our unconscious mind will see, hear, feel, smell, and taste a lot more than what we are consciously aware of.

"Float like a butterfly. Sting like a bee. His hands can't hit what his eyes can't see."

– **Muhammad Ali**

How is this possible? It is because the unconscious mind has an expansive neural network. In the scientific community, it is often said that the neural network of the unconscious world is more prominent than every dust particle in every star, in every planet, in every solar system, and every galaxy in the entire universe. Suffice to say, there is an enormous amount of possibilities with our unconscious mind that science is only now beginning to understand.

Your conscious mind is linear. However, your unconscious mind has the processing power of 2 million bits of information per second. Your unconscious mind is similar to how a server farm can process parallel data. **Thus, the power that lies in the unconscious mind is so enormous that you can heal any illness or transform any negative behavior.**

Overcoming addiction without tapping into the power of the unconscious mind seems almost impossible, as the unconscious mind always wins. One of the reasons why people struggle with addiction is that, consciously, they want to quit, but unconsciously, they cannot, because they get some reward from the bad behavior. It is important to note that whenever there is a battle between the conscious and unconscious mind, the unconscious mind always, always wins!

All your beliefs act as a filter under the control of the unconscious mind. Anytime you generalize something, or you believe something, it goes into your autonomic nervous system, and there's no way you can run away from it, because it filters out the information. The way you currently observe the world, alters the unconscious mind.

In short, the unconscious mind is not conscious to you, yet it is everything that's happening internally, and everything that you're aware of externally to your senses, without being conscious. I realize that sounds confusing, so let's break it down:

- **The unconscious mind is not conscious to you** (Remember, it controls 95% to 99% of your brain.).

- **The unconscious mind is everything that's happening internally** (It controls all of the automated bodily functions that keep you alive.).

- **The unconscious mind controls everything that you're aware of externally to your senses** (If you are fighting a cold, your nose may continue to run, which you are aware of because you have to keep blowing it.).

- **The unconscious mind works without you being conscious of it** (An excellent example of this is how you can pick up a pen. You don't have to tell your hand to pick up a pen. You think that you need a pen to write, and your unconscious mind does the rest, which proves that there is seamless cooperation going on between the conscious and unconscious minds.).

Similar functions take place when you are driving. When you're driving, you are not aware of specific actions that are operating from your unconscious mind, as it takes care of these details for you so that you don't drive into a wall.

That's the power of your unconscious mind. You're not running the show—it is. The concept of free will, to a conscious mind, is non-existent, unless we become partners with the unconscious mind.

For instance, they asked Muhammad Ali how he was able to anticipate when his opponent would attack, as he would often lean back to avoid getting hit, and he would dance around the ring with his infamous *Ali Shuffle*, which would often catch his opponent off guard. In Ali's mind, he was able to slow down the match and run imaginary circles around his opponent. The power of his visions enabled him to become so quick that he was able to get behind his opponent and look back, which helped him to know which direction the punch was coming from. Even early in his career, when he went by the name of Cassius Clay, he seemed to be two steps ahead of anyone else. I have developed a system that helps to train athletes to use this technique. It is so powerful that it can help transform a minor league player into a major league player, or a failing athlete into one that thrives.[31]

"Your unconscious mind expresses itself through feelings, habits, and sensations in your body (e.g., pain, light-headedness, muscle tension). So-called emotions, such as happiness and sadness, are the conscious mind's assigned labels to unconscious processes, such as an electrical or chemical reaction in the nervous system. The emotion is

31 https://www.macleans.ca/society/muhammad-ali-the-balletic-boxer/

experienced in the body as sensations; we nominalize the experience in the body, and talk about emotions, often losing touch with the true feeling."[32]

Because we cannot see the essential part of our mind, we are influenced by our past experiences that are stored in the unconscious mind. As such, good and bad representations from our past are stored in the unconscious mind. When we are reminded or triggered, the past image of that experience comes forth to our conscious attention. As the unconscious mind is habitual, it remembers to activate a physiological acute stress response, otherwise known as a *fight-or-flight* response, when a person is around the terrifying phobia stimuli.

In addition to our feelings and moods, our unconscious mind is responsible for an enormous amount of our functioning. We are utterly oblivious to how it impacts our cognition. How we can remember, store knowledge, learn, perceive, think, formulate instincts, or recognize language—all come from our unconscious mind.

If our unconscious mind is controlling the vast majority of our brain activity, then it is certainly doing more than controlling just our decisions, emotions, actions, and behaviors. Our autonomic nervous system, which is part of the peripheral system, is mostly unconscious, as it controls vital internal body functions and operations, such as heart

---

32 https://www.nlpacademy.co.uk/articles/view/understanding_your_mind_conscious_and_unconscious_processing/

rate, swallowing, breathing, lymph system, digestion, production of antibodies, and arousal. Miraculously, all this happens unconsciously.

Moreover, our motor learning skills and habits, which are learned and recalled, are memories of our unconscious mind, which allow us to walk, run, dance, eat, ride a bike, etc.

WHO IS IN CONTROL, AND WHAT TYPES OF RELATIONSHIPS CAN YOU HAVE

What is this unconscious mind? Is it our friend, or is it our foe? It's neither. It is just another part of us, which has an entirely different logic and motivation. The unconscious mind has its way of doing things, and it's not able to communicate in the language that we use. Therefore, without a common language, it seems that the unconscious mind is somewhat foreign to us.

How do you partner with someone, or something, that you cannot communicate with?

Well, since we store all of our memories, perceptions, and life experiences outside of our conscious awareness, the unconscious mind is malleable, open to our suggestions and conditioning. Therefore, if we embrace and create a unity with our unconscious mind, we facilitate its creative power to work with us as a partner.

We can consciously manipulate our auditory and visual senses in the Western world, and we can use them to easily communicate with our unconscious mind, as the conscious mind can visualize and hear things without having an image or sound present.

For example, if I asked you to imagine a pink elephant, you could use your internal dialogue by saying that you can do it. However, as our physical senses are strictly under the exclusive domain of the unconscious mind, we are unable to manipulate those easily. Therefore, using physical sensations is what we can effectively use to communicate with our unconscious mind.

To begin a relationship with the unconscious, we need to respect its autonomy and provide it with a channel that the conscious mind cannot manipulate.

Now I want to teach you how to communicate with your unconscious mind, as it is the single most powerful tool you will have to create a life that you have always wanted.

USING SIGNALS TO COMMUNICATE WITH YOUR UNCONSCIOUS

Since the unconscious mind cannot speak using our language, we cannot use it, as we can manipulate the process. Hence, to work with the unconscious mind, we choose to use physical sensation to communicate.

Begin sitting up straight with your feet on the floor. Relax your mind and close your eyes to open up some bandwidth from seven (plus or minus two) bits of info, as this will also help you to listen to what is happening in your body.

Next, do a body scan to make sure and to take note of any discomfort, pain, or sensations that you are currently experiencing. It's essential to make a note of these pre-existing issues so that you can compare it to later in the exercise, as this will be your baseline. Start with both feet on the floor, and uncross your arms and legs.

Take a deep breath, using four counts to inhale, four counts of holding, and 10–12 counts to exhale. The exhale should be long and drawn out, as it will assist your body with producing serotonin to calm your mind. Repeat this breathing technique three to four times. Then, with the same voice that you use to talk to yourself, say the following:

"DEAR UNCONSCIOUS MIND, I WANT TO COMMUNICATE WITH YOU. FOR US TO COOPERATE, I NEED YOUR HELP. I WANT TO UNDERSTAND HOW I CAN HELP YOU. IF YOU AGREE WITH ME, I WANT YOU TO GIVE ME A PHYSICAL SENSATION IN MY BODY THAT IS CONSCIOUSLY IMPOSSIBLE FOR ME TO REPLICATE. THAT WAY, I CAN BE SURE THAT THIS MESSAGE IS FROM YOU."

Now, wait for the unconscious mind to give you a sensation in your body. Very patiently and quietly, scan your body for physical discomfort or sensation. For example, you may notice your hand pulsing, or a burning sensation, or any other physical sensation that wasn't there before. This new sensation is your signal. Once you experience the signal, say:

> "DEAR UNCONSCIOUS MIND, THANK YOU FOR GIVING ME A 'YES' SIGNAL. I WANT TO CONFIRM THAT THE SIGNAL WAS FROM YOU. TO BE ABLE TO TRUST IT, CAN YOU PLEASE TAKE THE 'YES' SIGNAL AWAY."

Wait for the signal to go away. This is the first sign if the signal is real. Say:

> "DEAR UNCONSCIOUS MIND, IF THIS SIGNAL WAS REALLY FROM YOU, I WANT YOU TO GIVE ME THE EXACT SAME SENSATION FOR A 'YES' SIGNAL, ONE MORE TIME."

You test it one more time to get a second confirmation. Every time your unconscious mind wants to say "yes," you will experience this physical sensation. Next, say:

> "DEAR UNCONSCIOUS MIND, NOW THAT I KNOW WHAT THE "YES" SIGNAL IS, I NEED TO KNOW WHEN YOU DISAGREE WITH ME, AND I WANT IT TO BE VERY CLEAR. THEREFORE, I WANT YOU TO GIVE ME A 'NO' SIGNAL THAT IS A

COMPLETELY DIFFERENT BODY SENSATION, SO
THAT I HAVE NO PROBLEM UNDERSTANDING
IT. PLEASE GIVE ME A SENSATION THAT MEANS
'NO.'"

Then, sit and wait for the signal to come.

"DEAR UNCONSCIOUS MIND, THANK YOU FOR
GIVING ME A 'NO' SIGNAL. I WANT TO CONFIRM
THAT THE SIGNAL WAS FROM YOU. TO BE ABLE
TO TRUST IT, CAN YOU PLEASE TAKE THE 'NO'
SIGNAL AWAY."

Wait for it to go away. This is the first sign if the signal is real. Say:

"DEAR UNCONSCIOUS MIND, IF THIS SIGNAL
WAS REALLY FROM YOU, I WANT YOU TO GIVE
ME THE EXACT SAME SENSATION FOR A 'NO'
SIGNAL, ONE MORE TIME."

You will be surprised how eager your unconscious mind is to start communicating with you. I remember working with an executive whose signal turned out to be a slap across the face. We attributed it to his unconscious mind wanting to get his attention for a very long time. With being suppressed for so long, it seemed that the slap was appropriate.

Now you have a "yes" and a "no" signal to use when communicating with your unconscious mind. There is no chance for your conscious mind to intervene.

If you are unable to connect with the unconscious mind using this technique, begin a dialogue with it, using one of the following Three signaling methods. However, you must always start with the body scan and breathing exercise.

1. physical sensations (asking for a "yes" and "no" signal)

2. body sway

3. swing a pendulum or tea bag

BODY SWAY

Stand up, put your feet together, lock your knees, put your hands at your sides, look up, and bend backward. Imagine you are leaning back to stare at the stars. If you lean back enough, your physical body will start to feel unstable to your conscious mind. That sensation allows the unconscious mind to take control. The message for the unconscious would be:

"DEAR UNCONSCIOUS MIND, PUSH MY BODY OR SWAY MY BODY TO ONE SIDE FOR A 'YES' SIGNAL."

If you feel your body swaying to one side, make a note of which side it is, as this is now your "yes" signal.

Then repeat the process by saying:

"DEAR UNCONSCIOUS MIND, PUSH MY BODY OR SWAY MY BODY TO ONE SIDE FOR A 'NO' SIGNAL."

Once you have received both sensations, you can use this code to communicate with your unconscious.

SWINGING A PENDULUM (OR TEA BAG)

Hold onto a pendulum from the end of the chain/string, using your fingers, and ask yourself to open the hand. Your micro muscles will take over while you ask for a "yes" signal.

"DEAR UNCONSCIOUS MIND, PLEASE SHOW ME A 'YES' SIGNAL USING THIS PENDULUM."

And for a "no" signal:

"DEAR UNCONSCIOUS MIND, PLEASE SHOW ME A 'NO' SIGNAL USING THIS PENDULUM."

You can also replace the pendulum with a tea bag, necklace, or gold chain.

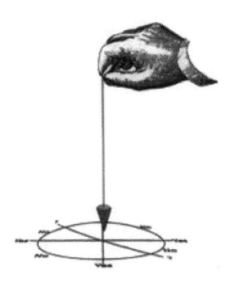

"A relationship with the one you love should never be built on control or dominance. Love them for them, and trust they do the same."

– John Cena

TAMING THE BEAST

There are two ways to think about your unconscious mind. You could consider it a beast that is illogical and does not have any intelligence, or like a horse that you want to tame.

You can tame your horse in two different ways: gently or aggressively. You can tame the horse by breaking it in, by putting a rope around the front leg and the back leg of the horse, causing the horse to begin kicking. The person will pull on the horse's front leg, forcing him to fall a few times. The horse will be so scared that he won't move, which allows someone to climb on the horse and sit on the saddle. But there is going to be a massive consequence for this, as this horse will never win a race.

That's one way of taming a horse. However, the other way is to use charm and to extend a hand of friendship. With this gentle approach, the trainer might hold a carrot or an apple in their hand, allowing the horse to get close to them. The trainer could then touch the horse's nose, pet his head, hug his neck, and bond with the horse, which allows the trainer or a rider to climb the horse gently.

This type of relationship is undoubtedly different from the first example, as a gentle connection with a horse can create a relationship that is viable, vibrant, generative, and fruitful. The former was that of a master and his conquered animal, with an unconscious mind that felt utterly defeated.

You can have either one of those relationships with your unconscious mind—you can either force or charm it.

For decades, psychologists, psychiatrists, coaches, or people in the know, have dealt with the unconscious minds of their clients. They wanted to tame the beasts, but this area was uncharted territory. So, they started forcing the unconscious mind, through repetition, mantras, and affirmations.

Those who are trying to force the unconscious mind by saying "do this, do this, do this," may sometimes have the unconscious mind respond to these commands due to the repetition. But an alternative way is to communicate with the unconscious mind using a shared vision, a designated auditory channel, and established yes and no signals through physical sensations as I have just taught you.

Once you have established your signals, you can ask questions to test it. For example, if you live in NYC, you can ask it if you live in Buffalo. If the physical sensation that you receive is "no," then your signaling system is working fine.

Now you can ask your unconscious mind questions, and say "give me a yes signal," or "give me a no signal." Since you have established relevant communication with your unconscious, and your unconscious mind's domain includes the conscious mind, your unconscious mind is the whole, and your conscious mind is a part of the whole. To understand the domain is where most people have a hang-up. So, it's best to get over it and know that there is a much higher part of you.

Logical thinking or logical understanding is entirely different, and the unconscious mind can have paradoxes that exist. For example, you can be sad and happy at the same time. You can be loving and have hate in your heart at the same time. But since the conscious domain is binary, which means it is either or, and since the conscious mind is the part of the unconscious mind, it means that with your conscious mind, you can act as a flashlight to point where you want to grab your attention.

So, we will set up a binary signal, using physical sensation or one of the other methods, for questioning and consulting with your unconscious mind. With this, you can ask the unconscious mind to become your ally and to get buy-in on anything you want to do. Why? Because when you are in sync with your unconscious mind, you will have the most potent force that is in your consciousness behind you, giving you what you desire in life.

"All the things that happen in our lives are tied to the unconscious. This is because it is, more than anything, the matrix of our repetitions."

– Gabriel Rolón

BUILDING A HEALTHY RELATIONSHIP WITH THE UNCONSCIOUS

In regard to your relationship between the conscious mind and the unconscious mind, as described with the taming horse example, you can have an amicable, loving, coexisting relationship with your unconscious mind, or you could be a master who beats it into submission.

With a loving friendship, your horse will come to your rescue when you fall. However, with a battered and bruised horse, it becomes insensitive toward your needs.

That is why having a good relationship and open communication channel with your unconscious mind is so essential. For instance, if you have a disease forming in your body, a friend would alert you so that you could get proper medical attention and care; but an enemy would let you suffer and die.

Your unconscious mind is not lacking intelligence; it has a different kind of knowledge. So, you need to have a relationship with it that consists of yes and no signals that you can use to ask your unconscious mind questions and to get buy-in from it on important life decisions.

You need to master the relationship with your unconscious mind, and then ask it to do certain things for you, such as bring ideas to your attention, or help you to build new skills. You can develop an incredible relationship with your unconscious mind that will enable you to create a powerful paradigm shift. Your world will undoubtedly be different once you have a relationship with your unconscious.

When communicating and building a relationship with your unconscious mind, there are effective ways and ineffective ways. Firstly, you need to be relaxed, which means you have to allow the hustle and bustle of the unconscious mind to subside so that you can open a channel of communication. Without the designated bandwidth, you will be unable to receive the signals.

Your basic bandwidth is fully utilized with the stresses and demands of each day. But when you relax and start to focus on your breathing, your body and mind will relax, and you will be more attuned and connected to your body. You will also unknowingly open up a couple of channels where you can start linking and receiving the sensations in your body.

People often become disconnected from their bodies because their channels are full and are coping with too many issues. However, once you open up the channels, you will begin to see your body heal from some ailments that it once suffered from.

It is helpful when communicating with the unconscious mind, to ask practical questions. For example, when wondering about whether you should marry the person you have been dating. A wrong way to ask would be, "Should I marry this person?" Instead, do the following:

"**DEAR UNCONSCIOUS MIND, WILL YOU SUPPORT ME IN FINDING FACTS ABOUT THIS PERSON SO I CAN MAKE A LOGICAL DECISION? WILL YOU BRING TO MY ATTENTION ALL HIS/ HER FAULTS?**" Then, once you know all the faults, you write them down. Then you say,

"**DEAR UNCONSCIOUS MIND, WILL YOU HELP ME TO ALSO BRING ALL OF HIS/HER GOOD QUALITIES TO LIGHT?**" Then, when you have both sides of the data, you will ask:

"**DEAR UNCONSCIOUS MIND, NOW WILL YOU HELP ME TO ANALYZE THIS INFORMATION IN A WAY THAT IS FAIR AND UNDERSTANDABLE TO ME?**" You could also ask:

"**DEAR UNCONSCIOUS MIND, COULD YOU SIMULATE AND SHOW ME WHAT IT WOULD BE LIKE LIVING IN A MARRIAGE WITH THIS PERSON?**"

5

Beliefs and Values

*"Your daily behavior
reveals your
deepest beliefs."*

– Robin Sharma

In this chapter, I want to reintroduce you to two essential concepts that have impacted your daily life since you were a child: beliefs and values.

Beliefs drive our actions, mannerisms, and thought processes, which means if we change our beliefs, we can improve our results in every area of our life.

Values drive human behavior, as they are key to motivation (e.g., the reason to get out of bed in the morning), relationships (e.g., trust, respect, empathy), and happiness (e.g., when we are living true to our value system).

BELIEFS

Merriam-Webster dictionary defines belief as "a state or habit of mind in which trust or confidence is placed in some person or thing; something that is accepted, considered to be true, or held as an opinion; something believed; and conviction of the truth of some statement or the reality of some being or phenomenon, especially when based on examination of evidence."

For the longest time, people believed that the Earth was flat, and they had confidence around that belief. Some people questioned what would happen to the others living on the other side. Would they fall off the edge? Some people also believed that Earth was in the center of the universe, and all other planets, including the moon and sun, orbited around the earth. However, this myth was later dispelled in the 20th century when other galaxies were discovered, and other models, including the Big Bang theory, were developed.

If you cannot touch, feel, see, hear, or have a way of proving that something exists, then it goes into the category of belief. All assumptions are beliefs, because there is no proof. And, as harsh as this may seem, beliefs are lies that we tell ourselves. With beliefs, there is certainty—that is all there is to it.

An idea, understanding, thought, or feeling that you are certain about is the technical definition of a belief.

In most peoples mind, there is no separation of fact from beliefs. The minute we believe it, we put it with the facts. Unless it is defined and/or predefined, whenever our belief becomes pervasive, it takes over reality.

Let's use poultry as an example. I can say that a chicken has four legs, without ever seeing a chicken, and that would be a belief. I don't need to verify it for it to be true.

As you know, in the real world, chickens have two legs and two wings. If I buy a chicken, I can count its legs and personally verify that it has two legs, not four. That is the truth. So, it's not a belief anymore. It's *knowing* that a chicken has two legs. Knowing is a verified practice that takes place in our minds.

Because we believe, we have confidence, which creates an emotional component, and we cannot separate fact from fiction. As such, we think that our beliefs are facts. The minute we believe something, we store it in our brain with other "facts." Certain things are not verifiable, which is why people confuse fact with fiction.

Twenty or thirty thousand years ago, the concept of fiction did not exist. However, since the advent of language, human beings have used fiction to make sense of their world. Fiction is the predecessor of belief, and belief is fiction with certainty attached to it.

Let us assume, when growing up, you experienced everyone around you referring to Hitler as a "great guy." Today, we all know that this is not true. However, if you had heard these messages ever since you were a young child, you would grow up with the certainty that Hitler was a good guy. So, if you met someone in the civilized world who said that Hitler was a bad guy or a monster, then you might get upset or start a fight. Now, let's imagine that you had power over nature. Then you could start a war.

This is an example of how wars are often rooted in twisted belief systems (e.g., radicalized version of religion). They all started with fiction, a lie, or an incorrect belief, with an added layer of confidence, making these beliefs quite powerful. They are invasive, ruling our lives and causing much pain for those around us.

Let's say that you believe that your mother is causing you pain. Unless she hit you, she cannot cause you physical pain. However, if you choose to react to something negative that your mother said to you, then you are choosing to be miserable or in emotional distress. Again, you are choosing to respond to your mother's words.

One's belief system is responsible for human happiness, sadness, success, and failure, because we filter our world through our beliefs. We have a small ability to process data with our conscious mind (i.e. seven plus/minus two bits of information each second). And the massive data that's coming at our unconscious mind is at a much higher rate (2 million bits of information each second). Therefore, we need to filter out and sample the data to understand what's happening. Our beliefs are used to help us generalize, store, and delete information so that we can deal with it.

We have seven, plus or minus two, conscious bits of information of attention, which goes as low as five and as high as nine bits open, depending on what mood we are in. Therefore, we often need to delete a significant amount of information. The information also needs to be generalized and put into a group that matches other data that we have previously stored due to our belief system (before this new information).

This type of thinking is the most significant human trap there is; if you believe something is true, it will persist by virtue of your belief. I know this sounds very confusing, so I will try to break it down for you.

Behavioral patterns and habits are passed down from generation to generation—even when the reason is not fully understood. These patterns are so pervasive in human consciousness, and can be very destructive in some cases.

It's like the famous story of a woman who used to cut the side of her roast every time she made it, because she believed that it was what she was supposed to do. After a while, her husband asked her why she did it, and she told him that her mother always cut the sides of her roast. Her mom did it because that's what her grandmother always did. So one day, the wife called her grandmother and asked her the reason for cutting the roast. Her grandmother told her that it was because she had a small roasting pan, and it wouldn't fit inside unless she cut the sides off the roast!

We tell ourselves lies, we make up stuff, and we believe fiction. It could be as simple as believing that Santa Claus lives in the North Pole, even though there is no scientific evidence to back up our beliefs. If you believe an idol is going to give you what you want, then it does. However, it's not the idol that gives you what you want; it's the belief in the idol that does its job.

Since our belief system is in charge of making sense of the reality around us, it will allow only pieces of data that fit the belief to come through. And that alone can form our reality, since we miss all the other pieces of data that does not meet this belief. It's sort of like you deciding that you want to buy a new car, and you believe that white cars are the nicest. All of a sudden, you will see a ton of white cars on the road. They were always there, but they were mixed in with other pieces of data (other car colours).

What types of beliefs are there?

BELIEF – IDENTITY

Anytime you say "I am," you are covering the real you. This type of self-identifying behavior is called *identity beliefs*. Often, these types of beliefs are not very positive because they were formed at a very young age. These identity beliefs are the mother of all beliefs. Anytime you say "I am," such as "I am fat," "I am ugly," "I am beautiful," "I am rich," "I am poor," etc., you are actually defining yourself as a being; and your *beingness*, which is your true essence, gets masked by something other than your pure beingness.

When we are born into this world, we come here with very little data. We are probably one of the only animals in the animal kingdom that come into this world and can't walk, talk, eat, or hunt without the support of a parent. So, we are learning machines that begin forming most of our beliefs at a high rate at a young age, often before the age of 5, which ultimately forms our identity. Our identity is something outside ourselves.

BELIEF – CAUSE AND EFFECT

Cause and effect is the belief that something causes a direct impact on something else. Often, people blame someone else for their mood or their mistake. They say things like, "You caused me to be embarrassed," or "You made me so angry that I broke the lamp."

But there is no true basis in this type of belief. Ask yourself what other people have to do with your emotions or behavior. If you say it and believe it, just because of its use in our language, your mind will believe this to be true, and act accordingly. As a result, you will live a life without any power or control, as other people are responsible for your actions or mood.

BELIEF – MEANING

People are meaning-making machines. We need to find meaning in everything we do and say, and everything that happens in our world. So, when we observe people behaving a certain way, we sometimes assume that it means something that it does not. Let's say that I failed at something, and I saw someone laughing. I then thought they were laughing at me. I believed that the other person laughed at me because they were happy about my failure. I created this fiction in my mind, with a sensation of confidence that this piece of data was true. However, they could have been laughing at something funny that they just read, which had nothing to do with me!

BELIEF – GENERALIZATION

Generalization is when you believe that everyone hates you or wants you to fail, or some other contrary assumption. These types of generalizations are pure fiction, as it is unrealistic to believe that you have no one in your life that supports or cares for you. To believe that you have only enemies, who mean you harm, is to live with false and harmful beliefs.

BELIEF – MIND READING

Do you hear yourself saying things like, "I know you're not in love with me," or "I know you're happy that I failed," or "I know you are not coming back to me?" These types of assumptions are based on fiction; but because they have a certain level of confidence behind them, they can cause serious problems with your relationships and other areas of your life. Assuming things about other people's intentions is never a good strategy to use in relationships.

BELIEF – COMPARISONS

Whenever you compare yourself to someone else, whatever you believe about that person, is not true. Let's say that you are 5'9", and you are standing next to someone who is 6'. You might believe that you are short. However, it is not true. When you are standing next to anyone that is shorter than 5'9", you would likely believe that you are tall, since everyone else is shorter than you. But, no matter what your belief, it's not true, because you have based it on the perspective, or viewpoint, that you had at that moment.

To recap, here are the best ways to identify if you are making up beliefs:

- Anytime that you say, "I am"

- Any concept where you have no facts

- If you have made up facts that you need to examine

To test whether your belief is true, you could ask your unconscious mind. If the answer is maybe or no, then it is a belief that needs to be examined to see how it is impacting your life.

Because we have so many beliefs, I like to use a tree analogy to demonstrate my point.

Trees have many branches and leaves that continuously grow. Even if you cut a branch or leaf off of the tree, it will continue to grow. However, if you cut the root of the tree, the tree will die.

This is similar to when you get to the root cause of an issue or a core belief. That is why I believe that many forms of therapy do not work for people. When you go each week, and the therapist asks you questions, you deal with your issues at the level of a belief. And, just as the leaves continue to grow back on a tree, by the time you return next week, you have more beliefs to work through with your therapist. So, even if the therapist has proper training, the therapy will not be effective.

Therefore, if you want to transform your life, you have to get to the core belief. Think about it. If your core belief were a snake, you would have to cut its head off.

The head of the snake, or the root of the tree, is the same, as they were formed many years ago, just as your core belief was. Your core beliefs, such as "I'm not worthy," are often formed at the tender age of three through five.

So, if you want to change a belief, or remove it, you cannot try to remove the belief that is negatively impacting you. Instead, you need to go deeper than that belief. On a tree, if you had rotten leaves, you would not just tear off the rotten leaves; you would go to the primary branch, the stem, and work your way to the root. And then you need to remove the entire tree. When you do this, you will never see that tree grow back again—just like your negative core belief will not resurface. You will be free to live your life unencumbered by beliefs that no longer serve you.

Believe it or not, going to the root of the tree, or your core belief, takes much less time than trying to resolve your beliefs one at a time.

It is important to note that once the tree has been removed, you cannot leave the space empty, as another rotten tree might grow. Well, this is the same as your core belief, as you cannot leave a space in your unconscious mind where the negative beliefs resided, as a bunch of noise and other negative beliefs may decide to take up residence in your brain!

If you planted a fruit-bearing tree, you would have fruit that produces for many years. These fruits represent the actions and reactions to issues in your life. So, every time you have a slight problem, you can ask yourself, "What belief do I have that would cause this behavior?"

You would then identify the belief so that you can start examining it. The minute you examine it, you will also see that this belief may not be valid. If it is not true, you will learn how to change the belief or turn it into disbelief.

Let's say that I have an anger issue, and my anger is toward my coworkers. I would ask why I'm angry toward my coworkers. I might believe that they are against me (wishing for me to fail). "They are against me" is a belief. That is the leaf-level belief that causes me to act negatively. So I would ask, "Why are they against me?"

I might respond, "Because they don't love me," or "Why don't they love me?" I might believe it's because I'm a bad person. Believing that I am a terrible person is the root of the tree, and also an example of a core belief.

To make sure that I have found the root, I would say, "What if I am a good person?" I might say, "If I'm a good person, would they not want to be with me?" I could continue to ask questions until I reached the point where I said, "I am," or "this causes that," or make a generalization. When you get to this point, you will know that you have discovered the root cause.

BELIEFS – CHANGING THEM

There are many ways to change your beliefs. One way to change your beliefs is by reframing them. You would ask if you have a positive intention. If you have the belief, "no one loves me because I am a bad person," then "I am bad" would be the core belief, and the positive intention for that is to be better and improve.

If you want to be better, but you continue to tell yourself that you are bad, despite how hard you work, you will be unable to create anything good in your life, and you will be unsuccessful.

The good news is that you do not have to discover your belief system alone! You can dialogue with your unconscious mind, and ask it to help you identify the belief that causes a specific behavior. By asking this:

"DEAR UNCONSCIOUS MIND, COULD YOU PLEASE SHOW WHAT CORE BELIEF IS THE ROOT CAUSE OF THIS BEHAVIOR." If the answer is yes, then you ask:

"DEAR UNCONSCIOUS MIND, PLEASE BRING IT TO MY CONSCIOUS ATTENTION NOW." As your unconscious mind is right alongside you, ideas will inevitably pop into your head. You can then ask:

"DEAR UNCONSCIOUS MIND, PLEASE VERIFY IF THE CORE BELIEF IS WHAT IS CAUSING THAT SPECIFIC BEHAVIOR." Once you have cornered the belief that you want to change, ask:

DEAR UNCONSCIOUS MIND, IF THE ROOT CAUSE BELIEF IS REPLACED, WILL IT DRASTICALLY CHANGE MY LIFE IN A POSITIVE WAY?" If the answer is yes, you can start working on that. Say the following:

"DEAR UNCONSCIOUS MIND, DO YOU HAVE A POSITIVE INTENTION FOR THIS BELIEF?" Using one of the communication modes we have set with the unconscious mind in the last chapter, look for an answer from your unconscious mind, by saying:

"DEAR UNCONSCIOUS MIND, I WANT YOU TO KEEP YOUR POSITIVE INTENTION, AS I'M SURE YOU HAVE A GOOD REASON FOR THIS POSITIVE INTENTION FOR ME. BUT I AM NOT ENJOYING THIS BELIEF, AS IT HURTS ME." Ask for a replacement belief that is ecological and positive for you, to be chosen by your unconscious mind. If the answer is no, then you say:

"DEAR UNCONSCIOUS MIND, IF YOU DON'T HAVE A POSITIVE INTENTION, WHY ARE YOU HOLDING ON TO THIS STUPID BELIEF?" Then plead your case. Tell your unconscious to change it to an ecological and positive belief. You can say:

"DEAR UNCONSCIOUS MIND, I AM A GOOD PERSON. I WAS BORN A GOOD PERSON." Reinforce it by way of repetition, making an emotional statement that is said with confidence and conviction. If it says yes, then you ask:

"DEAR UNCONSCIOUS MIND, CAN YOU FIND A NEW BELIEF THAT IS POSITIVE AND ECOLOGICALLY SOUND, AND REPLACES MY NEGATIVE BELIEFS?" If the answer is yes, say:

"DEAR UNCONSCIOUS MIND, FIND THIS BELIEF AND REPLACE IT. AFTER YOU HAVE DONE IT, GIVE ME A 'YES' SIGNAL." If you get a yes signal, then you can go back and examine the situation further. Say:

"DEAR UNCONSCIOUS MIND, AM I A BAD PERSON? I DON'T FEEL LIKE I'M A BAD PERSON. I AM A GOOD PERSON." Then you go and examine the branch-level belief that "nobody loves me." If you automatically come up with:

"DEAR UNCONSCIOUS MIND, WHY SHOULD THEY NOT LOVE ME? I'M A GOOD PERSON. MOST PEOPLE LOVE ME. SOME PEOPLE DON'T LOVE ME." Once you've got it, it is so important that you test each time to be sure the change has happened.

In short, this is one way of actually changing the belief system. Once you find it, you can always ask your unconscious mind to help you to change it. One way of changing a belief is by simply reframing it, by saying, "What's the intention behind this? Let's keep the intention and change the belief, and ask the unconscious mind to do it, because the unconscious mind can easily manage these types of requests.

ASSOCIATIONS – TO CHANGE BELIEFS

The other way to change the belief is through associations. Let's say that you had a belief, and now you don't believe in it anymore. In the past, you may have believed that Santa Claus was real, and now you believe that Santa Claus is not real. This is something that you believed, and you no longer believe; or you don't care anymore if it's real or not, because you have outgrown the belief.

When you think of the things you believe, say, "I'm a bad person, just like Santa Claus is real." You associate the negative belief with something you no longer care about. After you say it 10 or 20 times, it will lose its charge.

You can ask your unconscious mind to verify if a belief still exists or does not apply anymore.

If your unconscious mind says yes, then basically you're done, because your belief is gone. Then you can change, consciously, to something else. For example, you can change a belief that you are a bad person, to a belief that you are a good person, by simply associating it with something you have certainty with, like, "there is blood inside my veins." So, you would say, "I know that I am a good person, just as I know that there is blood inside my veins."

Beliefs are all lies that we make up in our mind anyway. For example, the belief that "I am ugly" or "I am beautiful." You can start making the mind lose its certainty of what that belief is, and then replace it with something else. It's important to replace the bad belief with a good belief, so that we don't leave its place empty within our unconscious, for a new bad belief to form.

If you believe you are destined to be rich, or you believe you're destined to be poor, which one do you think will have a positive impact on your life? They are both fiction. So, which fiction do you want to choose to have in your head? It's as simple as that.

Because beliefs were formed when we were children, and we believed everything our parents told us, we do not have an understanding that these beliefs are meaningless. They are just a bunch of beliefs that you can choose to do something with. You can change them, manipulate them, and make them exist, or replace them with something else.

After saying something bad about yourself, another way you can prove that you no longer believe negative things about yourself, is to repeatedly say, "I don't believe this."

The other way to get rid of your negative beliefs is to write them on a piece of paper and burn them. By burning the beliefs, you can create a symbol that shows that you do not believe in them anymore.

Can you think of something you used to believe that you don't believe anymore?

Let's use the belief that Santa Claus is real, for an example. That's a good one because most Christians believed that Santa Claus was real at some point in their life, but they stopped believing as they grew older. If you still believe that Santa Claus is real, where inside your mind would you see that picture? What would that image be? Would it be a picture or a movie?

Would the image be in black and white, or in color? What would the shape and distance be? You would examine your belief that Santa Claus is real, and file it in your mind. Then you take a negative belief, such as, "I'm ugly," and you cut it to the same shape and distance as your belief in Santa, and place it there.

Then you can do the opposite. For example, if you think you are a bad person, and you want to be a good person, say, "I know I am my mother's son. I believe, and I know to be true that I'm my mom's son." Take one of these positive beliefs and say, "I believe I'm a good person as strongly as my heart is beating for me to be alive." Visualize it. Where is the belief? Is it a picture or a movie? Create that image, and paste it over the negative believe. You can change that belief just like that.

Belief is the bullshit you say, which you have full confidence in. But the minute you take away the confidence from a belief, it is nothing more than gossip or fiction, and it has no leg to stand on. In other words, it has no more power over you.

"Open your arms to change, but don't let go of your values."

– Dalai Lama

VALUES

Values are beliefs that are important to you. We prioritize our values, and we unconsciously make them meaningful or not meaningful.

Ask yourself over and over, "What is more important to me than something else that I think is important?" Once you contextualize and compare your values, you will be able to see what is truly important to you. Do you value a healthy relationship or wealth?

To achieve this end, write down everything that is important to you. List ten to fifteen values, and ask, "Which value is the most important to me?"

List them again, with the most important one first, then the second value of importance, and so on. You may have to rewrite your values a few times. This process will demonstrate which values you hold most dear to you.

Since we know that beliefs are something that you make up (i.e. fiction), and that they continue to change over time, values become the sorting mechanism that helps us to define what's truly important to us. Values are the criteria that we create.

It's not the value that is important, but instead, it is their sequence that is important. Let's say that somebody has health and fitness as their first value. Their second most important value is happiness, the third value is relationships, and the fourth value is community. This person believes that these four things are most important to them, while another person may think that financial abundance, success, status, and luck are their most important values.

What is important to you? If you say that relationships are important to you, but you have bad relationships, then I know that relationships are not an important value to you; or the value you indicate may be your number one priority, but you believe that you are not worthy of love.

If there is an incongruence present, it means that there is either a conflict between values, a conflict between beliefs, or a conflict between values and beliefs. The conflicts are the problem. How do I know this? Because, if you have no conflicts, you will get what you want out of life. It is imperative that we remove these conflicts, as they eat away your inner power, and they waste your energy.

One other way to know what is important to you is to write down a list of ten to fifteen different values, and then take two at a time. Take the top two, and ask yourself, if you could only have one of these two, which would you rather have?

Let's say that you have love and happiness at the top of your list. You would need to choose between the two values. Then you would take the winner and compare it to the next value on the list. You continue to do this until you are left with only one value, and the most important values to you are at the top.

"Belief is the bullshit you say, which you have full confidence in. But the minute you take away the confidence from a belief, it is nothing more than gossip or fiction, and it has no leg to stand on."

– Aslan Mirkalami

6

Time Traveler

"Nothing puzzles me more than time and space; and yet nothing troubles me less."

– Charles Lamb

TIME AND SPACE

We have all seen movies like *Back to the Future,* where the protagonist goes back in time, changes one thing, and creates a different future. This type of ripple effect, in chaos theory, is referred to as the Butterfly Effect.

With the Butterfly Effect, one small change can create more significant changes to occur. The idea started from a weather prediction, with the concept that a butterfly, flapping its wings, would cause a hurricane or typhoon to take place halfway around the world. Of course, the single act of a butterfly flapping its wings cannot cause world disasters.

However, the concept is easy to believe, just as a pebble, hitting and skipping along the top of the water, can create a ripple effect. The seventh bounce of the pebble would not have occurred without the first bounce.

The Butterfly Effect was in play the day I met my now ex-wife. I was having my car serviced at the dealership, and my now ex-wife was with a friend who was looking to buy a car. I saw her in the dealership showroom, and I couldn't take my eyes off her.

Now, imagine if I hadn't been there that day, or if she hadn't entered the showroom, or if I hadn't entered the showroom while waiting for my car to be serviced. Imagine if I hadn't talked to her, or asked for her phone number—well, my life would be quite different.

Our meeting was the beginning of a lovely courtship, and we had a marriage that produced two beautiful children. The lifetime of experiences that we had may not have happened if we hadn't met. Makes sense, right?

Perhaps I never would have married, and I might have made different career choices, which might have forced me to travel. Maybe I would have abused my body with cigarettes, drugs, alcohol, and junk food. I could have been surviving a miserable life, with vices, and I could have been just one double bacon cheeseburger away from a cardiac arrest! There is no telling where my life would have ended up!

But luckily for me, the Butterfly Effect was alive and well the day I met my now ex-wife. We met, we spoke, we dated, we fell in love, we married, and we later Separated.

OUR MEMORIES

Our mind has a perfect memory of the past. Our unconscious mind has a considerable memory of every little detail that has ever happened in our lives. However, we are unable to access all of the memory because it is not useful.

For example, my now ex-wife and I had a giant house with eight bedrooms. When we sold our home, we couldn't even believe how much stuff we had accumulated over the past 16 years. We had to get rid of about 90% of our belongings. We had truckloads full of stuff that I auctioned off. Then we moved into our new, 4,000 square foot home, and we still had two huge trucks carrying all of our remaining stuff. Plus, we had to fill up the entire basement and the garage with extra things. There was a lot of stuff!

The hoarding of clutter is precisely what happens with our memories. Well, two things happen. The memories sink into the unconscious mind, and it gets forgotten—just like our cluttered home. Everything we brought into that home disappeared and got lost somehow. But imagine if one of our possessions was radioactive, or something was omitting some poisonous gas, and we were living in the house among these dangerous chemicals. What would have happened to us? We all would have been poisoned, and we would have never known the cause, because the gas was slowly killing us.

Just as poisonous gas would kill us slowly, our memories are events in the past, and how we relate to them has a similar but non-deadly effect on our lives. Because events took place in the past, our mind is looking at our history, which includes painful experiences and hurtful things that loved ones said or did to us. All of these painful memories become frozen in time, as the past hurts imprint on our unconscious mind, affecting how we feel about ourselves in our present lives, and subsequently impacting how we treat others.

However, we are not aware of the powerful force that painful memories have on our current and future lives. Because behavioral change takes place at an unconscious level, we need to go there to resolve the issues.

Just as using visualization techniques will help you to create a mental image of a future life that you want and love, it will also help you to imagine *yourself* in the future, so that you can overcome blocks that might get in your way.

If you ask somebody how they would look when they are 90 years old, some people would immediately have a mental image that pops into their mind. If you could capture their mental image and show it to them when they turn 90, they would be shocked at how similar it would be to when they see themselves in the mirror.

However, other people are unable to see a mental image of themselves at age 90, because they probably believe they will not survive that long. Being unable to see yourself in the foreseeable future is unfortunate, because that message is being encoded into your unconscious mind.

I told you about my father, who repeatedly said that he did not want to live to see 100 years old if it meant being ill. My father said that he wanted to be healthy, and to live to age 60. That's precisely what happened. Just before his 60th birthday, my father was diagnosed with cancer, and died a short time later. He couldn't see himself living past age 60, and so his unconscious made sure that he didn't.

"The most important thing in changing human behavior is the person's motivation."

– Milton Erickson

TIME TRAVELLER

What if we could travel into the past and heal past wounds, and help to repair our future by releasing negative emotions and unwanted beliefs? Can you imagine how powerful that would be?

Because people don't change consciously, transporting back to periods in our lives where problems first arose, can help us to release the effects of past negative experiences, and help us to change our programming, such as the way we think, feel, and behave.

If we can visualize, then we can use timelines to access our past and future.

Again, humans unconsciously store memories in their unconscious minds, as well as a vision of what direction they are going in, and what is going to happen in the future.

Therefore, we need to know how to access this vital data. If I said to you, "Point to something you're going to do next week," you are going to point to a direction either in front of you or to the side of you.

How do I know this? It is because there are all types of timelines. Most people point in front of them when referring to their future, while others will point to their right. If I asked you to point toward a space, for something you did last week or last month, where would you imagine it to be? You would likely point to your left side or behind you. Some people might look up to the future, and down to the past.

Timelines

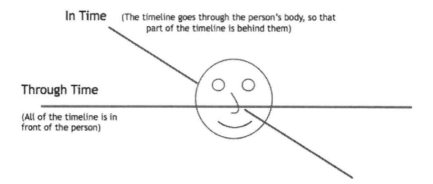

In Time (The timeline goes through the person's body, so that part of the timeline is behind them)

Through Time

(All of the timeline is in front of the person)

Timelines determine what type of personality you are. For example, if the time is going through you (from back to front or front to back), you are thinking in time, which means you prefer to code your memories from the front (present) to back (past).

As people perceive time differently, it makes sense that our flow of time would be different as well. For example, some people code their memories from left to right, or right to left. *Through-time* people think that the past is on their left, and the future is on their right. For them, time is continuous and uninterrupted.

Again, there is no wrong or right way to consider—we are just different.

"We all have a timeline. Most of us don't live like we have a timeline."

– Steve Gleason

TIMELINE EXERCISE

I want you to stop what you are doing and sit comfortably in a chair.

Think about what you did last week, and what you are going to do next week, and next month, and then point to it. Now draw an imaginary line, either going through your head (from back to front) or passing in front of you (from left to right).

Now you can close your eyes and detach yourself from your body. Imagine that you are looking down at yourself as if you are a fly sitting on the ceiling or a wall, six feet above your head, looking down at yourself.

You're sitting on a chair over there, and you see yourself in the present moment. With the past behind you or to your left, I want you to move back to an event that happened a few days ago, and look down. You see yourself down there going through that event, and then you remember something that happened a week ago, and you move back along that timeline to that event, seeing yourself down there going through that event.

Now move back to one month, and look at yourself down there; go back three months, and do the same thing. Now go back to one year, and repeat the same process. Then go back three years and then five years. Then go back to significant life events, such as graduations, births, deaths, and marriages, and repeat the same thing, and go back as far as you can remember.

You will see that the line keeps extending, allowing you to witness different episodes in your life. You will see yourself in high school, in elementary school, and preschool. You will see yourself interacting with friends and family.

Some people can go back to the ages of two or three, and others only to the age of nine or ten. However, some people are unable to remember their childhood at all.

No matter which way you are on that timeline, I want you to (even if you have to use your imagination) go far back, to infancy, and see yourself as a young child. I want you to keep going back, imagining yourself as a baby, at the moment you were born, just coming out of the womb. Then I want you to see yourself as a fetus, and then the moment that the sperm entered the egg—and that's your beginning. Believe it or not, you can go back that far, and see it in your mind.

If you believe in past lives, you can go back beyond that. You can jump beyond your birth, become a spirit, and land in a former life. For people who don't believe in past lives, your birth is your beginning.

That's where the soul enters the body, or the sperm meets the egg, and we become a human being.

Now I want you to come back to the present, as fast as you can, witnessing everything in front of you as if it is in fast forward. Then go to the future by thinking of some of the things you will be doing. Think of things you have planned for tomorrow, and then think of what you will be doing next week. Then go forward a month, then a few months. Continue to go ahead into your future. See your next birthday, later next year, then five years from now. Then go to your 80th birthday, and then go to the last day of your life on this Earth.

You will see a little light coming up, but do NOT enter the light. Just go near it. Then I want you to look back and see all the life that you have lived, and then come back to the present. These past and future experiences are coding inside your mind already, and now you can access it.

Our life is like a cannonball, moving through time and space. When you shoot a cannon, it has a trajectory, as it is very predictable. Similarly, our past has a great influence on our direction and future, as it somewhat determines where we are going. But we can also influence our path, and we can change the course by leaps and bounds. The fact that we know that we are coding the past and future, gives us the ability to do just that—but in a much bigger way.

Now I want you to look at another axis as you're looking down at your body, seeing yourself in the present moment. Is your future in front of you or to your right? Is your past behind you or to your left?

I want you to look and see that the timelines are there, and that you can go slightly higher. Instead of six feet above your head, go 15 feet, then 50 feet, then 250 feet. You will go higher and higher up, and you will notice that your entire perspective changes.

I want you to go up as far as you can go, until you see the beginning of your life and the end of your life, but where you can see all of it in one view, as a big giant line. Continue higher so that the entire line becomes as long as a yardstick. Then I want you to go up high enough so that it's like an inch in front of you. Keep going up until you see the whole line become a little dot and then disappear.

You are now able to see the beginning of life and the end, in a single point. Then I want you to come back down until it covers the entire horizon. Continue to come down until you see the beginning of your life and the end of your life. Come all the way down to a point where you are again six feet above your body.

Look down and see yourself sitting on that chair. See yourself the way you are now. You are now back to the present. How did that feel? Were you able to see your past and future close up, and from a far, safe distance?

Congratulations! You are learning the basics of working with a timeline. Moreover, taking a journey into your past and future helps you to rewire your negative thoughts and behaviors that are holding you back in life.

"The only reason for time is so everything doesn't happen at once."

– **Albert Einstein**

HOW THE UNIVERSE UNFOLDS INTO YOUR LAP

Now you have discovered two axes or tools for accessing your past and future.

By using these two axes, you can go back and forth in your life, anytime. So, you can become an actual time traveler.

Your conscious mind may not remember your travels, but your unconscious mind will. More importantly, since we have opened up a communication channel with your unconscious mind, we're going to use your unconscious mind to take us places, by using this axis as a resource.

As you drop into your body, you see that the future is in front of you or to your right. It is unfolding itself into your lap. You can move through that timeline like a zipper that you can open and close. You are just basically traveling through that course in time.

It is destined for you, as your unconscious mind has decided its limitations based on past experiences, your ancestor's teachings, school, and society. You have become who you are. Your unconscious mind is programmed, and it knows if it wants to keep you safe, happy, loved, and excited, or miserable, poor, and disliked. Your unconscious mind has control of your belief system, which is the filtration system for you to become aware of things consciously.

Since you filter out the 99.99% of the information, seeing only through your beliefs, then you can create the life that you want to live. However, it is not you building your life. It is your unconscious mind that leads you there, which is very difficult for most people to accept. As our unconscious mind works, it has much to say about where we are and where we will be.

That is why people who want to lose weight, or to give up an addiction, or to become wealthy, cannot achieve it. It's because there is a more significant force at play. You need to understand this force; you need to respect it and work with it. But most people do not do that. If we were consciously in charge of our heart beating, we would have been dead a long time ago. Luckily, our unconscious mind takes care of it for us!

"When you come to a fork in the road, take it."

– Yogi Berra

STANDING AT THE FORK

We are now at the point where we have devised an intervention tool that you can use. Your time machine (working with your timeline) can allow you to go in the past and change things there. Remember, when we change the way we relate to things from the past, and reverse them, we can feel a particular state.

Imagine for a moment that our unconscious mind is a horse that has seen a snake at a certain point in time in the past. Each time the horse gets to that point, he becomes spooked again by the snake. The horse will never want to go there again. Similarly, whatever has happened to you in your past—good or bad—has left memories in your timeline. Since emotions are controlled by our unconscious mind, these emotional triggers are the main reason we stay away from certain behaviors, or why we are compelled to do other behaviors. Our decisions and behaviors are the reasons we have ended up where we are now. We may be able to put temporary fixes on things in our lives, but soon, we will be back to where we began. That is unless the butterfly effect takes place, and it changes our current position, including the way we think and feel about the things that are happening to us in the future.

That is the premise of this work. Through the power of this type of time travel, and with the help of our unconscious mind, we can get our lives back on track. We can change things that currently hinder us in our lives.

Let's say that you smoke cigarettes, and you are unable to quit. Or maybe you are stuck in an abusive relationship and are unable to leave. I would tell you, "Look into the future, and tell me if you continue with this addiction or abusive relationship."

By looking five or ten years into the future, through the timeline, and seeing the negative consequences of your current choices, you are more likely to make better choices at this point in your life, to change the course of your future and to create a new life for yourself.

Let's try it. Look at your future, and ask yourself, "Where will I be if I continue on the same road?"

Using this timeline device, we can see the consequences of our choices. We do not make poor decisions because we are stupid; we do it because we are getting through the hustle and bustle of our busy lives, and we don't have the foresight of the consequences that we have created. We do not understand that what we do today impacts us tomorrow. It is not much more than an animal's ability to have foresight. The whole idea of using the timeline is for us to be able to construct a future that we are doing unconsciously anyway, and become conscious about it.

Fill in the blanks:

If I am doing this (i.e. negative behaviors) in a year, in five years, or ten years, my life will turn out to be (i.e. consequences). I deserve more. Therefore, I need to change course NOW.

"You can recover from all that has happened to you."

– Sebern Fisher

ACCESS YOUR PAST TRAUMA

The other way to course-correct your future is by asking your unconscious mind:

"DEAR UNCONSCIOUS MIND, TAKE ME TO THE ROOT CAUSE OF THIS BEHAVIOR OR EMOTIONAL TROUBLE."

Let's say that I'm just a sad person, or I suffer from depression or addiction; or I have certain negative habits that get in the way of my succeeding in life. I can ask:

"DEAR UNCONSCIOUS MIND, CAN YOU TAKE ME BACK TO A TIME THAT IS THE ROOT CAUSE OF THIS BEHAVIOR?"

Then, untangle the emotional state connected to the context, and make the right decision.

Your unconscious mind knows exactly the time you made the wrong decision, when your limiting belief was formed, or when you experienced a trauma. The problems that you are currently dealing with formed because the trajectory that your life was on was hijacked. Therefore, you can go back to that exact time and witness it from above.

Now, using the vertical axis, if you are not comfortable, you can go a little bit farther out. Look at yourself from almost a mile, and see yourself being beaten up, or experiencing the trauma that holds you back in life; or see yourself hurt or disappointed by something that someone did to you.

You can manipulate the Butterfly Effect and have access to your future life through your unconscious mind, because you can construct it safely. You can see yourself making future behaviors and making future decisions.

When you have access to the past, and access to the future, on a well-selected time frame, then you have full control of your life.

Please make sure that you practice this timeline technique a few times, since we are going to use it a lot in the next few chapters.

"A journey of a thousand miles must begin with a single step."

– **Lao Tzu**

REORGANIZATION OF YOUR TIMELINE FOR OPTIMIZATION

Your timeline is going through you: Behind you is the past, and in front of you is the future. With the continuation of time going through you, you can organize your time.

Let's say that if your timeline is in front of you, and you want to change it, then you should put it in front of the future. By placing the issue in front of you, you can shift it, like placing a latch on a door. You are permanently locking it in.

So, you can now look at the world with the future in front of you, and the past behind you, rather than your future to your right and your past to your left, which will enable you to reach beyond your goals.

Using timeline techniques such as this can create powerful changes in our lives. The goal is not to block or forget our painful pasts, because we can, of course, learn from all of our past experiences. If we can learn to discard the emotional baggage but keep the lesson that the painful experience taught us, then we can use them to help us make better decisions going forward.

At a minimum, our past negative experiences help to build character, strength, and resilience. The way that we see our past greatly influences our present feelings and behavior. By reducing the negative charge that our painful past has on us, we will be able to build a future that we truly desire.

"Your life will change the moment you become more committed to your dreams than your comfort zone."

– Dan Mendilow

7

Healing Yourself

"We live in a culture that believes that most of what we do is done consciously. However, most of what we do, and what we do best, is done unconsciously."

– John Grinder

This chapter pulls everything together that you have learned so far, and teaches you how to heal yourself. The past chapters have been putting the foundation and lessons you need to have to be able to do this work.

You have learned to become a time traveler by rising above yourself and traveling back into the past. You have also learned how to use a signaling system to help you to communicate with your unconscious mind. The method I recommend the most is an unconscious physical sensation, but the other ways (e.g., the body sway system, pendulum, or muscle testing) are just as good.

Knowing how to travel back in time, and seek answers from your unconscious mind, is the basis of this work.

If you picked up this book to clean up the mess in your life, and to live the life you truly want, then you will want to follow the exercises in this chapter.

Think of a situation that you are truly unhappy with. It could be painful feelings that are holding you back in life—or worse, a harmful habit or addiction that is toxic to your health and wellbeing. You could be holding onto anxiety or excessive anger, which wreaks havoc on your nervous system. Or you could be living in constant fear or suffering from debilitating sadness or depression. Or perhaps you lack wealth or positive relationships. You could be overweight or obese, and concerned about what the excessive weight is doing to your health.

"Create the things you wish existed."

– Unknown

REVISITING YOUR TRAUMA WITH YOUR LITTLE SELF TO HEAL YOUR LIFE

To fix yourself, you need to create a context and framework so that you are clear about what you want your unconscious mind to work on. Since weight and obesity are prevalent issues in society today, let's use that as an example to communicate with the unconscious mind. You would say:

"DEAR UNCONSCIOUS MIND, WOULD YOU BE WILLING TO WORK WITH ME ON THE CONTEXT OF BEING OVERWEIGHT?" If you get the yes signal, you know you're going to have to continue with the dialogue. But if the answer is no, then you need to ask:

"DEAR UNCONSCIOUS MIND, IF THE ANSWER IS NO, WOULD YOU BE ABLE TO PREPARE YOURSELF WITHIN A COUPLE OF MINUTES?" If the answer is yes, then stop for a few minutes and allow the unconscious mind to prepare. Then ask if the unconscious mind is ready to continue.

To work on the issue of being overweight, you have an opportunity to tackle the problem. Often, women who carry extra weight are emotionally protecting themselves from men, as it allows them to hide their beauty from plain sight. For others, the additional size helps them to feel more powerful. An overweight adult could have been bullied as a child, or abused by their parents, and the larger size can make them think that the additional weight or size provides a protective shield from the world.

As a child, they may have said to themselves, "If I were bigger, no one would mess with me."

But as a grown-up, the unconscious mind cannot differentiate between saying, "I want to be big" and "I want to grow up." The unconscious mind could have misinterpreted the wishes of the child, and delivered a life of being heavy.

Continuing to use obesity as an example, you would say:

"DEAR UNCONSCIOUS MIND, IS THE ROOT CAUSE OF ME BEING OVERWEIGHT BECAUSE OF SOMETHING IN THE PAST?" The answer will most likely be yes. If it is yes, then you ask:

"DEAR UNCONSCIOUS MIND, CAN YOU TAKE ME THERE?" The answer will most likely be another yes, in which case it can take you there. But if the answer is no, you can ask:

"DEAR UNCONSCIOUS MIND, CAN YOU LEARN TO TAKE ME THERE SAFELY? If it says yes, wait for a couple of minutes. Then say:

"DEAR UNCONSCIOUS MIND, DID YOU LEARN HOW TO TAKE ME THERE SAFELY? If the answer is yes, ask the unconscious mind to please take you there. But if the answer is no, ask the unconscious mind to find the resources to take you there at a later time.

You go back on top of the timeline (e.g., six feet above you), going younger and younger where an event is happening. Most likely, it is a traumatic or painful event. As a young child, any trauma in that time will have an impression on you. You look back into the far distance and ask the unconscious mind one more time:

"DEAR UNCONSCIOUS MIND, IS THIS THE ROOT CAUSE OF EVERYTHING THAT HAS HAPPENED TO ME? IS IT THE REASON I AM OVERWEIGHT? IF I CHANGE MY FEELINGS ABOUT THE WAY IT HAPPENED, USING THE BUTTERFLY EFFECT, WILL IT IMPACT THE FUTURE IN A WAY THAT I COULD START LOSING WEIGHT?" If the answer is yes, you have witnessed the trauma from a safe and far enough distance, and also from the beginning to the end.

Next, go back to the beginning, before the time of the beginning of the trauma, and let's call it your *happy time*. Introduce yourself to your younger self. You have to do this as realistically as possible. It's like showing up back then with your current look, and more importantly, your acquired wisdom. For example, if it were me, I would go down and say, "Hi, it's Aslan. I am you from the future. I am here to help you."

Little Aslan would be surprised, so I would tell him, "Everything is going to be okay. Whatever is going to happen is just a little bump in the road. I'm going to be here to help you. I'm from the future to help you. Something is about to happen that might look to be traumatic, but I'm here to support you and be with you to help you through it."

Before you are about to witness the trauma from the third position (as an adult), think about what you would give your younger self. What resources, feelings, emotions, or support could your little child need that would prevent him/her from feeling further trauma from the situation? Speak to your little self, and as you get ready, open up your arms to the Universe and pull in what you need. For example, pull in good energy, love, support, resources, and anything that is needed to help your young self.

Again, pull positive strength down from the Universe, and let it into your body as much as you can. Load every cell with the energy that you need, and store it inside of you. Next, bring the energy and hand it to your little self. Comfort your little self by holding his/her hand. Tell him/her, "I'm going to hold your hand, and I'm not going to leave you alone. Don't worry. Be calm and confident; we are going through this together."

By doing this, you can go through trauma as a supportive adult. A trauma that was unbearable for you as a child, you can handle, as you have prepared and have loaded the resources needed to deal with this properly. The role reversal that happens in the unconscious mind is so powerful that your unconscious mind doesn't understand what's happening. You were a victim, and now you are a savior—the last memory you have is of you as the victor.

The first time you endured the trauma, you were a young victim, powerless to fight or escape. But this time, you experience the trauma as a victor, to help the victim. This process rewrites the entire code, which has been embedded in your unconscious mind.

As you move through the traumatic event, you hold the hand of your little self, to make sure he/she is feeling supported, loved, and protected. Guide your little self to pass through a few moments of the traumatic event until he/she reaches safety. Let's call it the *safe place*. Then look at him/her as an adult, and ask if he/she is okay. Did his/her spirit survive intact? If the answer is no, then repeat this process.

This time, bring more resources with you, and be there with your little self until he/she ends up in a safe place and has entirely survived, with spirit intact. Then you take your little self by the hand, and walk with him/her through time.

Continue to walk with your little self to the present, and never let him/her go. Walk past all of the other times that repeated this traumatic event over and over again, until you get to the present moment, where your little self is your current age. You will notice, with each walk through the little self's timeline, and as he/she grows older, your little self will begin to look happier, more at peace, and at a healthy weight.

Ask your little self, "Would you want to be one with me. Would you like to join me?" If the answer is yes, then you will hug your little self, and allow him/her to enter your body. Inside your adult body, you'll have a slimmer body, and you will say to yourself, "It is now time to drop the extra weight. It is time to become my true self, because everything has shifted, the Butterfly Effect is in effect, and I want the Universe to change me physically to what I am now spiritually. Ask the unconscious mind:

"DEAR UNCONSCIOUS MIND, IS THIS OKAY WITH YOU? CAN YOU DO IT IN AN ECOLOGICAL WAY THAT IS NOT GOING TO HARM ME?" It is essential to ask this question, as you could be harmed if you lose a hundred pounds very quickly. Say:

"DEAR UNCONSCIOUS MIND, I WANT YOU TO DROP ME TO THE WEIGHT THAT IS SAFELY INSIDE ME. I AM A SKINNY PERSON. I NEVER REALLY HAD TO GAIN WEIGHT, BECAUSE THOSE THINGS DID NOT NEGATIVELY IMPACT ME." Your inner layer, where your spirit or soul resides, never really had to gain weight to protect your outer layer. Say:

"DEAR UNCONSCIOUS MIND, I WANT YOU TO TAKE MY PHYSICAL APPEARANCE AND MAKE IT THE SAME AS MY SPIRITUAL APPEARANCE—THE WAY IT SHOULD BE." If you get a yes answer, then start dieting and exercising to lose the weight. Your unconscious mind will work with you to support your weight loss goals. You will need to make a conscious effort to burn calories and build muscle.

You will need to go through the weight loss process for the last time in your life, as your excess weight will not return. You would use this blueprint for revisiting the root cause of your issue, taking you back through the sequence, witnessing it from your position, and providing support and resources to your little self.

We merged to become one, and asked the unconscious mind to use the new version as the physical copy. You can use your unconscious mind to heal yourself, as it will naturally help you to repair any issues that you have in your life.

"The unconsciousness of man is the consciousness of God."

– **Henry David Thoreau**

BEHAVIORAL-BASED METHOD OF HEALING:

To work with a method that is more behavioral-based, you need to understand that every behavior has a positive intention behind it. There's a very famous saying: "The road to hell is paved with good intentions."

Let's say that I believe I am too shy, and I want to change it. What is the purpose of being shy? There's always a positive purpose behind it.

Let's say that if I get angry, there's a positive purpose behind that behavior. Perhaps it is defending myself, where I use my anger to stand up for myself now.

Good intentions do not equate with getting what you want in life. It means that you have only good intentions. But physically, in this world, it has to be translated the right way. Often, the unconscious mind has to find a way that's easy and reachable, forgetting about ecology or appropriateness. Commonly, alcohol is consumed to bring happiness or a state of relaxation, just as some people smoke cigarettes because they say it makes them feel relaxed.

The intention of smoking, drinking, or getting angry is not those things. Often, the purpose of our actions is very different than our actions or behaviors. So, you need to go to the intention level to stop these behaviors. You can ask the unconscious mind for help. Say:

"DEAR UNCONSCIOUS MIND, DO YOU HAVE A POSITIVE INTENTION?" Most likely, it will say yes. However, if it says no, you need to ask it a series of questions, because it does not have a positive intention to the signaling system that you have developed in a previous chapter. If the answer is no, ask the following questions, and wait for the signal:

"DEAR UNCONSCIOUS MIND…"

- **"DO YOU UNDERSTAND WHAT'S HAPPENING TO ME BY DRINKING ALCOHOL?"** Wait for a signal!

- **"DO YOU UNDERSTAND THAT THIS IS COSTING ME MY HEALTH?"** Wait for a signal!

- **"DO YOU UNDERSTAND THAT IT IS COSTING ME MONEY?"** Wait for a signal!

- **"DO YOU UNDERSTAND THAT IT IS HARMING MY FRIENDSHIPS AND PERSONAL RELATIONSHIPS?"** Wait for a signal!

- **"DO YOU UNDERSTAND THAT IF I CONTINUE LIKE THIS, I WILL BECOME ILL?"** Wait for a signal!

- **"IF YOU HAVE NO INTENTION, THEN WHY WOULD YOU CONTINUE TO HURT ME LIKE THIS?"** Wait for a signal!

- **"COULD YOU STOP HURTING ME?"** Wait for a signal!

- **"CAN YOU PLEASE CHANGE THIS BEHAVIOR THAT I AM UNHAPPY WITH?"** Wait for a signal!

- "I WANT YOU TO CHANGE MY NEGATIVE BEHAVIOR TO ONE THAT IS POSITIVE AND ECOLOGICAL. I WANT MY DRINKING PROBLEM TO BECOME A JOY AND LOVE OF DEEP BREATHING AND MEDITATION, OR PLEASURE FROM WATCHING COMEDY MOVIES WITH FRIENDS, INSTEAD." Wait for a signal!

At this point, you are making a deal with the unconscious mind. Now, let's go back and start over. Ask:

"DEAR UNCONSCIOUS MIND, DO YOU HAVE A POSITIVE INTENTION?" If the answer is yes, ask the following questions, and wait for the signal:

"DEAR UNCONSCIOUS MIND..."

- "I DON'T WANT YOU TO LOSE YOUR POSITIVE INTENTION. I WANT YOU TO GET WHAT YOU WANT. BUT DO YOU UNDERSTAND THAT THIS IS NOT GOOD FOR ME?" Wait for a signal!

- "I WOULD LIKE YOU TO CONSIDER FINDING BETTER SOLUTIONS FOR ME. WOULD YOU HELP ME OUT?" Wait for a signal!

- "WOULD YOU BE ABLE TO FIND TWO OR THREE ALTERNATIVES—ECOLOGICAL OPTIONS— THAT WILL REPLACE MY OLD UNHEALTHY BEHAVIOR?" Wait for a signal!

- "WOULD YOU BE ABLE TO SWITCH THEM, SO I DON'T GET ANY DISTURBANCES LIVING WITH THESE UNHEALTHY BEHAVIORS?" Wait for a signal!

- "WOULD YOU HELP ME SO THAT I CAN GET THE BENEFITS OF YOUR POSITIVE INTENTIONS, SO THE RIGHT BEHAVIORS ARE ASSOCIATED WITH IT?" Wait for a signal!

- "PLEASE, CAN YOU DO THAT NOW AND GIVE ME A POSITIVE SIGNAL?" Wait for a signal!

- "IS IT DONE?" Wait for a signal!

Now, go and test to see if the process worked:

- If you are a recovered alcoholic, ask yourself how you feel about your previous favorite drink?

- If you were overweight, think about your problem foods, over which you have had no self-control in the past.

- As a smoker, imagine a stressful day—are you craving a cigarette?

If these vices feel and sound like crap, you have worked through another way to heal yourself from these negative forces in your life.

> *"Sometimes you don't realize the weight of something you've been carrying until you feel the weight of its release."*
>
> **– Unknown**

COMBINATION METHOD

Now we will try a method that combines the two techniques. You would ask the unconscious mind to help you deal with the issue in your life. Ask the unconscious mind to take you to the traumatic event in your life. You would ask the unconscious mind if it is the root cause of it in the past and the unconscious mindset. You would rise above yourself six feet, and allow your unconscious mind to travel, taking you back to the moment of the traumatic event that was causing the problems in your life.

As you witness the traumatic event, you ask the unconscious mind if it is the root cause. Go to the end of that event, to the safe zone.

Go down and associate yourself, and become you, the little child. Step into the body of your little self, and merge with the child. As you do that, I want you to roll everything back. It's like playing a video in reverse. Rewind in a faster than normal speed, where all of the words and motions are backward.

Instead of someone beating you, they are taking their beatings back. Everything is going back until it reaches to a happy time. As soon as it arrives at a happy time, you jump back to the safe time again, and roll back to the trauma again. Repeat this four or five times.

Now, roll forward through the trauma, and look to see if it causes you to feel any anxiety or sense of discomfort. If you have lost all the pain and the emotion of the traumatic event, you can blast the imprint that was left behind. Now you can step and roll forward through your timeline, to the present, entirely associated in your body.

> *"The unconscious mind works without your knowledge, and that is the way it prefers."*
>
> **– Milton H. Erickson**

REPLACING YOUR SELF-IMAGE WITH VISUALIZATION

Let's say that your self-image is a source of a lot of negative behaviors and feelings. We refer to that self-image almost a thousand times a day. So, can you imagine the negative impact it unknowingly has on us each day?

Because you look at that self-image in your mind, it impacts how you think and refer to yourself. You will end up becoming the image in your mind. However, you can place a positive image of yourself overtop of the negative image, and snap it in like a Tupperware lid.

First, make up a new image of the way you wish to be. If you are overweight, then have yourself look slim and sexy in your new image. Then make your new image overlap the old image. Do it fast, five to eight times, and then look at the image in your mind. You will see the new image of yourself.

You can continue this every day, or even make an altered picture of yourself. I used this technique myself. I was very strong in my legs, but my upper body was not strong, so I took a picture of a great looking guy, from a magazine, and photo-shopped my face on him. I used it as a screen saver to reinforce the work I did.

If you are overweight, imagine that you look skinny when you look in the mirror. Repeat this five or six times a day until, when you look at yourself, you see a reflection of a healthy, robust, and fit version of yourself. Or, visualize yourself eating healthy and participating in sports activities instead of drinking alcohol and smoking at a bar.

Do this enough times, and eventually, your body will start moving in that direction. The body will start changing all parts of you to fit that new, healthy image.

8
Self-Image

"A strong, positive self-image is the best possible preparation for success in life."

– Dr. Joyce Brothers

CREATING A POSITIVE SELF-IMAGE

In the previous chapters, I've shared with you how you can change your limiting beliefs by communicating with your unconscious mind. Additionally, using time travel, you can heal parts of your past life that have been traumatic for you, impacting your ability to move forward. Another way to repair is to create a positive self-image for yourself.

I want you to think about your self-image. How do you see yourself currently? I don't want you to think about how you wish to be just yet. Often, clients who come to see me have read a lot of self-improvement books or have had some coaching. They give me a wish list, but a simple congruency check takes care of that.

For this work to be transformational, I need to know exactly where the person is at now, and where they want to go. It is like asking for a taxi to pick you up but giving them the wrong address. So, being realistic is essential. What is your current self-image?

What types of behaviors or habits do you have that you wish you could stop or change? I often ask my clients who suffer from negative self-beliefs, whether there was an image in their mind of the person that would have that belief. What kind of person would do things like that? What does this person look like in your mind?

You need to know how it looks in your mind in order to address and correct the problem. To do so, you need to make a smaller image, and place it on top, in the corner of the negative picture of yourself. Do this five to ten times, very quickly, and expand the positive image, and cover the old image. By repeating the process, you will have the new fixed image in your mind's eye. To test if the change has happened, when you look at your image, the new positive image should be the only image that you see in your mind. If it's not, you need to repeat the process.

> *"It is not what you are that is holding you back. It is what you think you are not."*
>
> **– Anonymous**

REMOVING THE ANCHORS THAT HOLD YOU BACK

Once you have created a positive self-image, you need to remove the anchors that are holding you back in life, by cutting them, as eliminating the anchors will enable you to move forward.

To do this, you need to be clear about where you want to go. Having an intention or purpose will keep you focused and moving in the right direction. Otherwise, any shiny object will distract you and pull you away from achieving your goals.

The best way to achieve this is to time travel into the future, and set time to all that you want.

Ask your unconscious mind if it can take you to a future time, where all of this is a reality. If the answer is yes, then ask for the unconscious mind to take you there now! If the answer to the question is no, then ask if it can pull all resources necessary to do that. Then, once you are looking at a time in the future that all this happened, go inside the image and feel it out, and make sure it feels good.

From the future, look back to the past, to see that you already have everything you want. Make a note of what significant steps you took in your life (and when) to get you to the place where you are now. The great thing about looking back from the future is that your unconscious mind is not able to differentiate between created reality (the work you are doing here) and the actual reality (your life as it has already transpired), which is why this technique works so well.

Can you imagine being able to repair some of the relationships you contaminated, and opportunities that you squandered because you didn't believe you deserved greatness?

I wish I knew about these powerful tools when I was in my twenties. I wouldn't have made the mistakes that I made. Being able to look back on your timeline, and to visualize your possible future from inside your mind, is a gift.

Having the hindsight from the future, and witnessing the consequences and repercussions of your decisions, provides you with the freedom to create the life you always wanted!

You become a witness of your life, and you change what needs changing. Your behavior will change, your beliefs in your abilities will be renewed, and your zest to embrace every moment life provides you with will feel as if you won the lottery.

Let's say that you are not happy about your weight, and you believe that you are always going to be fat. You can challenge that belief by asking, "I'm fat compared to whom?" And you can change that belief through several techniques that I have shared with you. Now, to change your belief, say to yourself, "I am as slim as anyone else." Remember, you can break any of the beliefs that have held you back, and then create a new belief that supports a new healthy behavior.

Think about what kinds of things a thin person does. Maybe they participate in dance competitions, or run marathons. Make those healthy types of activities a goal for yourself. Say, "I'm going to do this activity," and you immediately start to move your body to release all of the pent-up energy that you had stuck inside you. Now your positive energy is moving toward the new goal, and they are both moving toward the new direction that propels you to success.

"Defeat is a state of mind. No one is ever defeated until defeat has been accepted as reality."

– Bruce Lee

STATE MASTERY

State mastery is getting in charge of your feelings by merely writing down what you're feeling, three or four times a day, and then changing it.

Let's say that you're happy, but you think you could be happier. You can go from happy to jubilant to ecstatic to stoked, or any other positive, exciting adjective you can think of.

You can push your feelings by simply asking your unconscious mind to help elevate your emotions. It is cheating—but it works! Say:

"DEAR UNCONSCIOUS MIND, I'M FEELING STAGNANT, STRESSED, AND ANXIOUS. CAN YOU CHANGE THIS TO ECSTASY?" And if you get a "yes" answer, say:

"DEAR UNCONSCIOUS MIND, GO AHEAD AND CHANGE IT TO ECSTASY RIGHT NOW." Then, all you have to do is sit back and wait five minutes. After five minutes, you will feel ecstatic, as your entire biochemistry will have shifted to a new euphoric state.

The unconscious mind does this for you from a chemical point of view, by adding pheromones and serotonin into your body. You wouldn't need a reason if you got your unconscious mind on your side, as it is the substantial chemical factory in the world!

State mastery can also help people who struggle with drug or alcohol addiction. I use this technique with my addicted clients, as I can help them to achieve the same feelings they would get if they had just consumed their vice of choice, yet they are completely sober. To do this, you say:

"DEAR UNCONSCIOUS MIND, CAN YOU REPRODUCE THE EFFECTS OF DRINKING OR DRUGS." If the unconscious mind says yes, which will almost always be the case, you then say:

"DEAR UNCONSCIOUS MIND, GO AHEAD AND PUT ME IN A DRUNK OR HIGH STATE." Within two to five minutes, you will experience the same effect that you would have if you were high on substances, but without taking the harsh chemicals. More importantly, you will have control, as you can make the sensation last as long or as short as you want.

All you need to do is ask the unconscious mind if it can help you, and when it says it can, you tell it to go ahead and do it, and to give you a signal when it's done.

You can also control how drunk or high you feel, by asking the unconscious mind to increase the effect of the altered state for you.

In this book, I have not kept any secrets or held anything back. Any of the techniques that I use with clients within my elite coaching practice, I have provided for you. Clients have spent lots of money with me. But you now have all of the tools necessary to make lasting changes in your life.

You do not have to follow chapter by chapter—but you do need to make sure that you learn the basic principles, like signaling and time travel.

Belief changing is another tool, and the only prerequisite for it would be to get the signaling down. I've shown several ways to change your beliefs.

The only thing you need to do now is to set your intention on what you want to change, and to get your unconscious mind on your side, which means establishing a signal for yes and no. You can make an infinite number of changes. People who communicate with their unconscious mind can do almost anything they want.

"It is no good getting furious if you get stuck…keep thinking about the problem but work on something else."

– Steven Hawking

CHANGING NEGATIVE BELIEFS

We always have beliefs we don't believe in anymore. Most people get stuck and lose control with their beliefs, because once they find something to be true, they see the world through that lens, and they are not able to recognize that this is just a facade.

Since all beliefs had a beginning when they were formed, you have the power to change them. There was a time in the past when you made a specific conscious or unconscious decision to believe certain things to be true. Therefore, you need to return to that place in order to change that belief.

Let's say that somebody believes that they are ugly and unlovable. If they ask their unconscious mind if it is true, the unconscious mind will likely say yes, and prompt them to the time in their life when the belief first formed.

Your unconscious mind will often block painful experiences from your consciousness, to protect you. Therefore, if you have negative beliefs that you want to change, you need to ask your unconscious mind to take you back to that time, before the decision was made to believe this to be true. By doing this, you go to a point in the event, which takes place just prior to when you made the decision. This is a pivotal time, as you have the power and ability to make a new decision, changing your belief automatically.

> *"The ego, however, is not who you really are. The ego is your self-image; it is your social mask; it is the role you are playing. Your social mask thrives on approval. It wants control, and it is sustained by power because it lives in fear."*
>
> **– Deepak Chopra**

MELTING THE EGO

After I have a significant breakthrough, I express love for the good, the bad, and the ugly.

All human beings have a dark side or shadow, which is the basis of the ego, where we hide parts of ourselves and pretend they are not part of us. Instead of hiding parts of yourself that you are embarrassed or ashamed of, what if you started to love ALL PARTS of you? How lovely and liberating would that feel?

One way to achieve this is to stand in front of the mirror, for five minutes each day, and love every part of you that you see. While locking eyes on your image, repeatedly say the following:

"I love you because…(say a good thing)."

"I love you because…(say a bad thing)."

"I love you because…(say an ugly thing)."

After 10 or 15 days, you will find that you won't care anymore. You will become very comfortable with the attributes that you were hiding. And, after 30 days, you will have unlocked your ego, and you will no longer be bound by it.

How this looks in your life is that you won't care what people think of you anymore, or you won't try to pretend to be someone you are not. All of that drama is exhausting! Just think of the newfound energy you will have, just by being you!

Melting your ego will be one of the most liberating gifts you can give yourself!

"You can't stop insane people from doing insane things by passing insane laws."

– Penn Jillette

CRAZY PASS

While working with a former client, I discovered the need for something that I refer to as a "crazy pass."

One day, a client of mine called from Vietnam. He was in love with a Vietnamese girl, who was half his age, and they were having a baby together. He was hysterical and not making a lot of sense. He kept saying that his wife was crazy, and he called her horrible names, which I dare not repeat. He said he was going to come back to Canada.

I asked him if a *sane* person would marry a woman half their age, who lives halfway around the world, and have a baby with this woman, whom he barely knows. Then I asked him if he thought his wife was sane or insane. I told him that if she was crazy, she deserved a *crazy pass*.

What do I mean by this? I knew that she could behave as "crazy" as possible, and he would continue to love her anyway.

Think about the Diagnostic and Statistical Manual of Mental Disorders (*DSM*–5), which medical doctors and psychiatrists use to diagnose mental illnesses. The DSM has been used for years to make it easier to diagnose people with some form of mental illness. It seems that each new addition that they publish, lowers the diagnostic thresholds for existing disorders, and adds new disorders for which people can be diagnosed and medicated with powerful psychotropic drugs.

So, in laymen's terms, it means that we are all crazy, with our mental illnesses, in some way. Therefore, if most of us are insane, why not give out crazy passes?

Politicians who irritate you? Give them a crazy pass. Neighbors that drive you nuts? Give them a crazy pass.

My hope is that rather than blaming each other for things we do or don't do, why not give each other a crazy pass so that we can move on to loving and respecting each other? I think that this alone could resolve a lot of humankind's problems.

People are crazy, and they will act crazy. Don't expect anything else. By using the crazy pass, it eliminates the power that people have over you. So, instead, let's give out crazy passes to the whole world, and understand that no matter who you are talking to, he/she has their own history of trauma, pain, rejection, and scars—just like you!

"It is in your moments of decision that your destiny is shaped."

– Tony Robbins

DECISION MACHINE

What if you could have a decision machine in your head that would always guide you to the best decision possible at the moment? What would it be worth? Well, there is a way! By partnering with your unconscious mind to create a decision machine, it is a great way to feel empowered with the decisions you make from this day forward.

To create the decision machine, think about the decisions you made in the past. If you think they were good decisions based on your results, you can use these to calibrate your machine. Then you can do the same with bad choices that you know you made in the past. Say:

"DEAR UNCONSCIOUS MIND, DO YOU AGREE THAT THIS WAS A GOOD DECISION?" Then bring the next right decision, and repeat the question. Continue this process a third time. Now you have three examples that you can calibrate for good choices.

Next, repeat the process, asking about your bad decisions.

Can you calibrate and find out what the common ground between the good decisions was? If you get a "yes" answer, ask: **"DEAR UNCONSCIOUS MIND, CAN YOU CALIBRATE AND**

FIND OUT WHAT THE COMMON GROUND WAS ON THE BAD DECISION?" Continue the dialogue, and ask:

"DEAR UNCONSCIOUS MIND, CAN YOU BUILD A DECISION MACHINE FOR ME THAT AUTOMATICALLY DECIDES WHEN SOMETHING IS A GOOD DECISION OR A BAD DECISION?" If you get a "yes" response, proceed to ask your unconscious mind to go ahead and build this decision machine, and to tell you when you are done.

In five minutes, ask your unconscious mind if it is done, and then you can begin to test it with decisions that you need to make. But first, check it with questions that you know are not rational.

For example, say: **"DEAR UNCONSCIOUS MIND, I WANT TO JUMP FROM A FIFTH FLOOR BALCONY. IS THAT A GOOD DECISION?"** If you get a "no" answer, ask examples of bad decisions.

Then try examples of good decisions. Say: **"DEAR UNCONSCIOUS MIND, I WANT TO STUDY FOR MY EXAMS BECAUSE I WANT TO GET A GOOD MARK. IS THAT A GOOD DECISION?"**

Now you can put your decision machine to the test with real-life questions.

185

What you've done here is calibrate a good decision unconsciously. You want your unconscious mind to build a process to help you to make decisions instantly, by seeing which one is closer to yes or no.

Continue this decision machine process for four to five weeks. You will make decisions that are profitable and helpful in your life.

I have introduced you to different tools and methods you can use, but the most important thing to learn is how to communicate with your unconscious mind using the signaling process.

Once you can communicate with your unconscious mind, you will be able to change the wounds, trauma, beliefs, addictions, and dead-end paths that have haunted you throughout your life.

9

Putting It All Together

"Until you make the unconscious conscious, it will direct your life, and you will call it fate."

– Carl Jung

GOAL SETTING

Imagine being able to change your feelings, beliefs, or theories about events or traumas that have stopped you in the past from fulfilling all of your dreams and goals. Doesn't that sound amazing?

To do this, you will need to look to your future to create the life that you truly desire. Using the timeline, you can go five to ten years into the future, and see, hear, and witness everything you want to.

Start by creating an image from your future of how you want to be living. Make your future as perfect as possible. It's essential to have a clear vision of the kind of person that you would like to become.

You are going to experience the future, seeing yourself in the third person. While you travel through your futuristic sightline, you will experience the kinds of success in areas of relationships, business, success, wealth, and health.

Let's say that your goal is to become very wealthy—a multimillionaire. Instead of focusing on the millions of dollars, think of the kind of person who would easily make a million dollars, or in this case, millions of dollars.

Instead of focusing on specific goals about the company or the products, think only about the kind of person that you would need to become in order to achieve your financial goal, as this will broaden the base and cover a lot of other areas in your life where you can create success.

Think about what type of person runs a multi-million dollar business. What is it about them that makes them so successful? What kind of lifestyle do they lead? Do they work 80-hour weeks? Are they a good parent or spouse? Do they have other interests? Once you have a strong sense of what it takes to become a multimillionaire, it will be easier for you to visualize yourself as this type of person, which will help you achieve your goal.

Once you have this clear image in your head, I want you to walk through it and experience it in the first person. Observe the multimillionaire. You are walking through aspects of your mind where you will set your intention to create this type of success, and to become this type of person. As you set your goals, you will experience what it feels like in your body to achieve them. You are experiencing it as if it has all happened for you. You feel powerful, driven, and grateful. You feel unstoppable. All of these thoughts create an overwhelming sensation in your body, and it feels 100% real.

From your future, you turn around and look back at the present moment. As you look at anything that is out of place, or at hurdles you need to overcome, you prepare for your journey back toward your present. And as you walk or slide back toward your present, you will deal with any obstacles, missteps, or missed opportunities that come your way, and you will look for anything that needs to be taken care of. See yourself addressing these issues.

Come back to the present, and stay present with thoughts and feelings. You are a conqueror! You are the slayer of your dreams! You are the captain of your ship!

To fully activate what you just experienced, repeat this exercise several times. As you do this, you will code your unconscious mind to go with you in the direction of your goals and dreams.

> *"Practice daily, because the quality of your practice determines the caliber of your performance."*
>
> **– Robin S Sharma**

HIGH-PERFORMANCE PRACTICES TO CEMENT YOUR EXPERIENCES

By performing this technique over and over again, you are telling your unconscious mind what you want, where you want to go, and how you want to be.

Next, for 30 days, I want you to participate in high-performance practices, such as writing down in detail everything that you want and see during your futuristic time travel. Everything you envisioned for yourself, and the type of person that you have become to reach all those goals, will soon be within reach.

Following the high-performance practices, I want you to do some mirror work for 30–45 days. Look in the mirror, and say, "I love you because...." Each time, come up with another reason that you love yourself. Do this for a couple of minutes, and then say, "I am enough because...." Each time you do this exercise, you need to lock eyes with your reflection, and state these affirmations with total conviction.

This activity will tell your unconscious mind that you are convinced that you are deserving and worthy of the goals you set. You are saying, "I love me, and I am worthy of my goals." It may feel uncomfortable to say these affirmations at first, but it will become easier over time, and you will eventually believe what you are saying. You need to say them with conviction, so if it takes you 30 days to get to that point, you should repeat the affirmations for an additional 30–45 days.

You can later have your unconscious mind take over this task for you, by saying:

"DEAR UNCONSCIOUS MIND, I'VE DONE THIS FOR 30 DAYS; WOULD YOU BE ABLE TO DO IT FROM NOW ON?"

If your unconscious mind says yes, then you will ask your unconscious mind: "Will you continue doing this every day?" And if your unconscious mind says yes, then you do not need to do it anymore.

"If you are going to ask yourself life-changing questions, be sure to do something with the answers."

– Bo Bennett

HOW IMPORTANT THIS LIFE-CHANGING WORK IS

I remember I had a client who came to me, and he had gone bankrupt at the ripe age of 26. He was looking for a job, and I said, "Look, I will work with you, and you can pay me after."

We worked together using the techniques outlined in this book, and within eight months, he earned a million dollars!

His story is not dissimilar from other clients that I have worked with, and whom then later made hundreds of thousands of dollars. I've worked with clients who have a criminal past, and who suffer from drug addiction. These techniques worked for them also. In fact, they were able to turn their lives around and make healthy, productive choices as a result of the work we did together.

I've had a client who suffered from serious depression for over 40 years. With his medical doctor's cooperation, he stopped taking his medication and began to experience a real life, unencumbered by darkness. Sometime after treating him, he wrote me a heartfelt letter, thanking me for giving him his life back. He was finally happy and feeling well.

I've had clients with various physical illnesses, from chronic nerve pain and migraine headaches, to debilitating fibromyalgia. Using the methodology outlined in the book, we were able to heal all of their ailments by communicating with their unconscious minds.

To be clear, I am not claiming to be a medical doctor. I am not a miracle worker, voodoo, or new age healer. I am an expert in working with the unconscious mind to help us to heal, fix, recover, and grow. My only goal is to help people achieve their best life. To do that, we often have to go back and repair some old childhood wounds; or, we need to create a healthy dialogue with ourselves, and especially with our unconsciousness mind.

To use this type of methodology, it's like working with a genie in a bottle. The genie is the unconscious mind that grants you your wishes. But the advantage here is that you are not limited to only three wishes. Your unconscious mind will continue to deliver, over and over again.

To work with this incredible system, it is imperative that you know what you want in life and what your core issues are. If you have these two areas covered, you can genuinely achieve any results you want to accomplish in life.

"Build your own dreams or someone else will hire you to build theirs."

– **Farrah Gray**

DESIGN YOUR DREAM LIFE WITH QUESTIONS

Not knowing what your issues are will undoubtedly get in the way of your success. But once you create the knowingness, everything starts becoming clear, as the unconscious mind will begin moving you toward achieving your goals at a rapid pace.

One of the things I ask my clients to do is to answer these four questions:

- If there were no limits, what would you want to do, or who would you want to be?

- If you had a hundred million dollars in the bank, what would you do, or who would you want to become?

- If you had only six months to live, what would you do, and who would you be?

- If you were to live forever, and you knew you would never die, what would you do, and who would you be?

The knowledge that you acquire from learning the answers to these questions will help you to set goals and, ultimately, move forward with your life.

Most people are looking at the world from a limited point of view. You will hear them say things like this:

- "I can't do this."

- "I don't want to do this."

- "I am not able to do this."

- "I don't have the money for it."

- "I'm not going to live long enough for this."

When you answer these questions, it brings forth what is most important and what is real to you. It is also a great indicator of what is demanding your attention at this point, and you will go much faster toward your goals.

Goal setting is very important. After you answer the four questions, you set out your goals into the future walk exercise.

I want you to feel exactly the way you would as if everything had happened. When you turn around, you will see all the flaws in your plan.

Then try to improve them. Walk back and look at those walls, and recognize where things need to go. The walls should resemble the milestones that you need to achieve along the way.

Let's say that you want to become a multi-millionaire, and you are an employee working for another company. One of your milestones would be to think about what type of business you want to own. Ask yourself what you are passionate about. What do you loving doing? So, ask yourself what you love and what you enjoy doing. Consider building a business around your passions and talents.

Review your ideas, and make sure that you use effective questions when working with the unconscious mind, to ensure that it has the capacity to provide you with answers.

Here are some great questions to ask your unconscious:

"DEAR UNCONSCIOUS MIND..."

- "HOW CAN I BECOME SUCCESSFUL IN MY LIFE?"
- "HOW CAN I BE AN AMAZING FATHER?"
- "HOW CAN I BECOME A BETTER HUSBAND?"
- "HOW CAN I BECOME WEALTHIER?"
- "HOW CAN I BECOME MORE FIT?"
- "HOW CAN I BECOME A BETTER TEACHER?"

One of your first goals is to create the questions that you want to ask, and design your routines to support the work you've already done, so that you can move forward.

It's like pasting your outcomes on your timeline, which provides you with more direction to continue doing the work. As you go forward, new powerful questions will be drawn to you like a magnet, as they will guide you toward the direction you want to go, catapulting you even further.

"Too many of us are not living our dreams because we are living our fears."

– **Les Brown**

10

Frequently Asked Questions (FAQs)

"We are what we repeatedly do. Excellence then, is not an act but a habit."

– Aristotle

Q: What if you have negative beliefs about yourself that you don't think can be changed. For example, how will your book help people who have suffered horrific childhood trauma, and as a result, they believe they are unlovable or unworthy at the core of their being?

First of all, deep, deep beliefs like these are core beliefs. Therefore, the first thing to do is to heal the trauma. Let's say that the person believes they are unlovable because of the trauma or injury that was done to them. We know what the cause of their negative core beliefs are, so we need to go back to that point of trauma, and go through the process that I outlined in earlier chapters on time travel.

It's best to go to a point in time that is before the trauma occurred. Then introduce yourself to your unconscious by saying your name and telling your unconscious mind that you are from the future. You need to forewarn the unconscious mind by saying, "Something bad is about to happen. But don't worry. You're going to survive it. Just hold my hand, and I'm going to give you love and protection."

Next, open up your heart and bring all the love from the Universe, and give this love and support to your little self. Ask your little self what he/she needs in order to not become traumatized by what is about to happen. Give it to your little self, hold his/her hand, and go through that trauma together.

After going through the timeline process, go back and test, and make sure that the trauma didn't impact your little self. Go back and clean up the scar, as if it never happened. The butterfly takes over, so you don't feel scared. And that belief will automatically be gone.

If the belief did not go away, but you cleaned up the scar, then you need to go to the point where you made that decision to have a self-limiting belief that is holding you back in life. Now, hold the hand of your little self, and say, "Listen, it's about to happen. Whatever happens, do NOT believe *this* to be true about yourself. Instead, make sure you believe *that* to be true." Define the difference in beliefs to your little self.

What's important to note is that if you do not believe the negative belief, and it doesn't form, then it can no longer hold you back in life. So, after going through the process, bring your little self to the present, and test it, and make sure to ask yourself, "Do I believe this to be true?" If the belief still exists, you will need to repeat the process until it clears. It's similar to the character in the *Back to the Future* movie.

I have used this process with dozens of clients who have come from bankruptcy, to earn millions of dollars later, and from people who were severely depressed and on all kinds of medication, to be free from drugs and feeling healthy. People get amazing results from this technique! I understand that this might be a bit difficult to do by yourself, so you can always contact me and use my services for private and group coaching. It is important that it is done correctly so that you can achieve the results you want.

By the way, the impact is paramount, because you're in control of a relationship with your unconscious mind, which means that you can use it as a tool to help you with all aspects of your life.

"Sometimes I remind myself that I almost skipped the party, that I almost went to a different college, that the whim of a minute could have changed everything and everyone."

– **Unknown**

Q: Tell me about how the Butterfly Effect kicks in. What does that mean exactly?

You see, the unconscious mind cannot differentiate between what happens and what is imagined to have occurred. For the unconscious mind, it is all the same. So, when you travel in time, and present a hypothetical situation in your mind, your unconscious mind reacts as if it happened in real life.

It completely recodes your unconscious mind. Therefore, you know it to be true, and if your knowledge is what you have gained out of this exercise, you can heal and correct all sorts of issues in your life.

The unconscious mind is not hindered with all the stress of dealing with that trauma and self-limiting beliefs. After the recoding, all of a sudden, the immune system becomes active, and starts functioning normally. You see, your immune system deals with current, important issues. It has its priority list, similar to if there is a shooting and the police arrive in two minutes; but for disputes or minor issues, the police sometime arrive hours later.

Your unconscious mind does not have the logic to recognize that the trauma happened 20 years ago. Any open loop means that anything that you have unresolved in your mind will continue to be worked on by the unconscious mind. It will stop only when you give it some closure. It is like the computer when you have too many programs open, and the operating system cannot handle it, causing it to behave strangely.

That's why a great exercise to do is to sit and write down any issues, fears, or concerns that you have in your mind. It is best to deal with these situations that are weighing on you. You may need to write a letter, send flowers, apologize—anything to close the open loops, as they are draining your resources. Alternatively, you can go back in time and work on them as described in the section on time travel.

> *"Most humans are never fully present in the now, because unconsciously they believe that the next moment must be more important than this one. But then you miss your whole life, which is never not now."*
>
> – Eckhart Tolle

Q: What if someone reads your book and is skeptical, and they think what you are doing is *brainwashing*. What's your response to that?

It is brainwashing!

Why do you wash your clothes? Because they need cleaning. You need to wash your brain too. But if you are doing the washing, you can have 100% confidence that the process of cleaning is to *your* benefit.

I mention this because brainwashing generally has a negative connotation. Unfortunately, some evil, mean-spirited people, with selfish intentions, have brainwashed others for their benefit. These negative people want to manipulate other people for their gain. And the people who were brainwashed were often not even aware of what happened to them.

To be clear, I am NOT teaching that. I am showing you to wash your brain of things that are holding you back in life.

Interestingly, when you learn these techniques, they protect you from others trying to brainwash and manipulate you for their gain. It acts as a protective shield or a tool that you can take out when you are dealing with someone who is especially toxic and manipulative.

You should be aware that if you are not happy with your life, you are particularly vulnerable to these types of bad people who can cause you harm. However, if you learn how to brainwash yourself, you will never allow anybody else to do it to you.

"Self-love is really a foundation for everything, and however you practice and express that is so, so important."

– **Solange Knowles**

Q: Are there any risks involved with recoding your brain? Is it possible to lose the good (e.g., confident, healthy) parts of your personality?

There are zero risks involved. The intention that you started this whole process with sets the framework for the work that you will do. When you open a frame and say which particular issue you want to deal with (e.g., weight loss, addiction, finances, relationships), it sets the boundaries of what is going to be impacted. Only issues within that framework will be changed or affected.

Moreover, everything you are doing is positive, as you are eliminating negative emotions, beliefs, and behaviors, and turning them into positive emotions, beliefs, and behaviors. So, given this, what could go wrong? Things could only get better for you!

Plus, this type of work is not ongoing. It has a beginning, a middle, and an end. And the work has clearly defined goals. I like to put in a solid 6–8 hours with my clients, as it gives momentum and a tremendous boost for things to move forward in my clients' lives.

But you don't have to do it that way. You can do it in small chunks. Whatever is comfortable for you, is the best way to approach it.

"A coach is someone who sees beyond your limits and guides you to greatness."

– Michael Jordan

Q: Is it better to do this work with a coach?

Look, if I told you that you could open the hood of your car and do everything yourself, and that you would get precisely the same results as a professional mechanic, I would be lying.

But you can get very close to doing the work on your own.

Using the mechanic analogy, imagine that my brakes need changing. I can probably figure it out by reading a book, or watching a YouTube video, all in the effort to save myself a few hundred dollars. But if I go to a professional who has done it a hundred times, he/she will not only do it correctly, but they will do it faster and more efficiently.

So, it is possible to do a good job using these techniques on yourself. You need to be diligent and go back and do it again.

But if you ask me if the result is going to be precisely the same, whether you are working on your own or with a coach you trust,, the answer is no. At least not the first time. Over time, you would get better with practice, as your relationship with your unconscious mind becomes more aligned.

You will get better at asking the right questions and reading the signals. Understand that you are welcome to contact me to get into one of my private or public programs, to ensure that you are doing the work effectively.

"Any fool can know. The point is to understand."

– Albert Einstein

Q: If I give a crazy pass to people who have hurt me, isn't that me saying it is okay for that person to continue to treat me this way?

Humans need to scratch wherever there is an itch. Our need to react when someone hurts us is similar. It's important to understand that when people behave poorly, it's about them, not us.

To know and understand this is liberating, as we will not get hurt from others' behavior. Remember, it's not because of anything you are doing or saying. Just think that this person is crazy, like 99% of the population. When you react to their "crazy," you are just scratching an itch, which makes it itchier. But when you ignore the bad behavior, the itchiness calms down, and the cycle breaks down.

"All you need is one safe anchor to keep you grounded when the rest of your life spins out of control."

– Katie Kacvinsky

Q: Do I need to revisit my trauma in my unconscious mind, to move past it? I'm terrified of doing this in case I fall apart and become no longer able to function. In other words, won't I become re-traumatized?

This is an excellent question. Before you revisit the trauma, you need to set an anchor or safe word. Besides, we always approach the trauma from a distance, up above and in a third position. If the trauma is quite significant, feel free to go a further distance, by allowing at least two layers of dissociation. Go back as far as you need to, so that you do not collapse into that memory. You can always contact me and enroll in one of my programs to get the best outcome.

"Your soul knows you are good enough."

– Elyse Santilli

Q: I want to try the technique of replacing a negative self-image, but I don't understand how to do it.

The easiest way is to identify your self-image first. You will likely see an image that represents something negative to you. What you want to do is to build a new image of yourself that is compelling, and that you can be inspired by. Now, imagine yourself pasting the new image over top of the old image. Repeat this process several times, until when you look at your self-image, you see the new image of yourself staring back at you. Now each time you do it, you are unconsciously referring to your self-image as this new positive self-image that makes you feel good about yourself. By repeating this process, you will start altering your life until you see a positive self-image every time you stare in the mirror or think about yourself. Ultimately, the goal is to have your unconscious mind and conscious mind see the same positive image of yourself.

"Visualization is the human being's vehicle to the future—good, bad, or indifferent. It's strictly in our control."

– Earl Nightingale

Q: Replacing your self-image with visualization techniques seems like it would be easy, except I keep seeing my actual reflection when I look in the mirror. How do I visualize something different with my eyes open, when I'm staring at my sad reality, in the face?

Think about your visualization techniques as if you are about to take a flight and go to an exotic destination. Thinking about something you desire as strongly as an exciting vacation, allows you to not only visualize an image, but you can engage your other senses.

What do you smell when you get off the plane? What are the sounds? Do you hear the hustle and bustle of a busy city, or the waves from an ocean, when you pull up to your hotel? Do you see how powerful that is?

Well now, imagine that you are going to wake up tomorrow, and you are going to look into the mirror and stare back at a person you are proud of. What do you see? How does it make you feel? Experience the *new you* as if it is your reality now. Your unconsciousness mind will interpret this experience as if it is real and true. When you repeat this type of visualization enough, your conscious mind will also experience *you* as a new positive, attractive, and powerful person, so that you can eventually manifest it all to come true.

TESTIMONIALS

Quick update: I finally left my old relationship this summer, became an empowered goddess! Met the man of my dreams on New Year's Eve, exactly EVERYTHING you had me right down last year all came to be in my life now, WOW.

- Aga :)

Hi Aslan, I wanted to thank you again for a very special day. It's hardly enough to call it transformational or whatever, it was such a rare and beautiful event in life to imagine that somebody out there would put the time and care into altering the future of another in such an impactful and conscious way. It means the world to me that this happened. I feel blessed to know you.

- Emily E

Hello Aslan. I am feeling sooo great! Why am I feeling sooo good. I am almost feeling guilty for feeling so good. Why is that? It's like it is too good to be true....

- Marietta

I had the privilege to meet up and do "the work" with Aslan about 3 weeks ago. I remember flying back from Toronto thinking "what just happened?".

I come from a spiritual/health and business background and have done serious heavy work on myself since my teenage years. Been there and done that with self-development, personal development and spiritual "awakening". You name it I have done it. With 5 different black belts in martial arts, national champion and not to mention 4 Near Death experiences I would say I know a bit about consciousness, being in the "zone", performance and getting results. However, I felt I was in a stand still in my life on many levels. something was not moving ahead or in the direction I wanted. Both physically, mentally and with business. I was stuck and needed a jolt. It came. After a huge wakeup call with 5 guys robbing me in my house, I ended up getting shot in the elbow with a shotgun. 5 months later in the hospital fighting a dangerous bacterial bone infection, I was told they need to cut out the whole elbow joint as it was 3 antibiotic resistant super bugs, you just can't kill. At that moment I knew I had to do something radically different to save my arm and my sanity and I started listening to my inner voice instead of the doctors' dark prognosis.

Few weeks later I was sitting in Aslan's office doing all kinds of exercises that seemed very counter intuitive for the mind and to my elbow and my situation in general. As a martial artist I however just thought well let the results speak for themselves and I just went along with it all. I only care about what works and seeing my best friend going through huge metamorphosis in the past 3 months when Aslan piqued my curiosity. I don't care about HOW it works only IF it works. In the plane home however, I was one big? and I know that's the perfect place to be. It's a sign something new just happened and the conscious mind has no clue what's going on. I still don't know what just happened 3 weeks ago. All I know is my bone infection is gone and I stopped all medications just to test out if it's for real. Bone is growing back slowly. I got shooting pains in fingers, I'm normally 100% numb. Doing things physically with my arm I couldn't do at all the first 6 months after the accident. All pain and swelling gone. I keep on doing the "homework" Aslan has given me and I see the momentum building up.

Business is looking very promising now after a long long time of stagnation. I see many small situations unfolding in very different ways than before. I got a new confidence in life. And people around me notice it. Phone calls, meetings etc. are happening in ways I have been wishing for in a long time. Amazing how when the inner terrain changes the outer follows every time. It's simple once you understand it as Aslan points out: conscious mind process 10 bit of information pr. sec. Unconscious mind process 2 mills. Who do you really think is in charge here? And how to tap into this power and regain conscious control? Once tapped in, there are no limits. I call Aslan my brain surgeon without a scalpel, as that's what he is to me. Putting things back in alignment after defragmenting the whole "hard disk". Now a bit of a warning. This is not done FOR you. You have to do this yourself. He is only guiding you. So be ready for self-effort and commitment. Aslan is no kinder garden summer camp. 3 weeks has passed while writing this. I cannot even imagine right now what 1 year looks like from now. I feel like I'm back on the horse and its finally paying attention.

- Joshua D.

Made in the USA
Middletown, DE
30 October 2019